Collected Essays
Volume One

Other book collections by Arthur Porges:

Three Porges Parodies and a Pastiche (1988)
The Mirror and Other Strange Reflections (2002)
Eight Problems in Space: The Ensign De Ruyter Stories (2008)
The Adventures of Stately Homes and Sherman Horn (2008)
The Calabash of Coral Island and Other Early Stories (2008)
The Miracle of the Bread and Other Stories (2008)
Spring, 1836: Selected Poems (2008)
The Devil and Simon Flagg and Other Fantastic Tales (2009)
The Curious Cases of Cyriack Skinner Grey (2009)
The Ruum and Other Science Fiction Stories (2010)
The Rescuer and Other Science Fiction Stories (2014)
Unusual Plants of the Galaxy (2014)
No Killer Has Wings: The Casebook of Dr. Joel Hoffman (2017)
These Daisies Told: The Casebook of Professor Ulysses Price Middlebie (2018)
The Price of a Princess: Hardboiled Crime Fiction (2020)

Forthcoming titles by Arthur Porges:

Collected Essays: Volume Two

Books by F. W. Thomas (from the same publisher):

Tales From Stonecutter Street (2010)
Star Turns (2011)
The Rising Sap (2013)

Books by Basil Wells (from the same publisher):

Final Voyage and Other Science Fiction Stories (2016)

Collected Essays
Volume One

Arthur Porges

Edited by Richard Simms

Richard Simms Publications

Contents

Introduction

In previous collections of Arthur Porges' writings that I have published to date, I edited selections of his short stories, taking in, for the most part, the genres of mystery, fantasy and science fiction. In addition, I compiled a book that I think provided a decent sampler of his best poetry.

And now, in these two volumes, the first of which you are holding in your hands, I have realized a long-held ambition to gather together a representative compilation of his finest essays and articles, which Porges penned quite late in life.

The majority of these essays appeared from 1986 to 1989 in the author's local newspaper, *The Monterey County Herald*. Porges was a resident of Pacific Grove, Monterey County, California for the last thirty-odd years of his time on this planet. The incumbent editor of the *Herald*, in the late 1980s period, was a big fan of Arthur's writings, and encouraged him to contribute what turned out to be over forty essays to the newspaper's Sunday supplement magazine, which at the time was called *Weekend*.

As an aside, I will note here that even after this stream of essays dried up, Porges continued to write poems, feature articles, social commentaries and letters for the *Herald* well into the early 2000s.

Along with those essays previously published (rather obscurely, I would say, especially if you weren't living in Monterey County at the time!) in this newspaper, a few of these pieces, which Arthur always described to me as "informal," were discovered by myself in manuscript form among the author's papers after he passed away. I am delighted to publish some of them here for the first time, with more to come in the next volume.

So what did Porges talk about in his essays? One hardly knows where to start, such was the broad scope of his interests and subject matter. I will note, at this point, for those of you who are impatient with my rambling introductions, that you can skip forward if you like, and see for yourself in the contents of this book what these essays are all about.

However, a few words on why I have elected to publish two separate volumes may be of interest. In the first place, there are rather a lot of them, so instead of one big weighty tome, two smaller ones seemed a good idea! But then I had to decide how to divide up such a large number of essays into some kind of order, be it thematic, or chronological.

This last proved largely beyond me, so varied are they in content. Nevertheless, for this first volume, I have compiled those essays where Arthur talked a lot about his personal life, alongside a few choice examples of his literary appreciations for writers whose works he admired reading as a young man. I have also included a few reflections on his passion for collecting books and all the minutiae of fascinating detail that comes with being a confirmed bibliophile.

The essays where Porges reminisced on incidents from his past are particularly fascinating to me. Various chapters of his life are covered in these. The schoolboy years, growing up in Chicago with three brothers and a widowed father; to his time with the U.S. Army during World War Two; to the early days of teaching mathematics at college; and finally recollections of various (sometimes amusing) experiences from his later life as a full-time writer living a bachelor existence in Southern California, through to his retirement in Pacific Grove.

A few of these personal memoirs, particularly those where the author looked back on his childhood in Chicago, make for quite intense reading. Arthur was so painfully honest at times about numerous incidents and happenings that it is apparent he was either downright ashamed of or decidedly embarrassed by them. Such vivid recollections are almost confessional in nature, and all the more powerful for it.

The tantalizingly brief glimpses of army life that we witness in pieces like "Hooked by the Major," are remarkable for their candidness. The author's period as an artillery instructor during the war was clearly formative, changing his outlook and influencing his development as a man.

Later memories, including those from his time living in a seaside house on the cliffs off the Big Sur, or learning to drive a car in his forties, or being one of the few perambulatory pedestrians in Monterey (Porges soon gave up the idea of driving a car!) in an area where few walk and most drive automobiles, are more often than not delightful, funny and, at times, poignant.

A number of the essays in this first volume defy categorization. One piece, which is not about Arthur's life, is "Love, Death and Mystery." Its inclusion here is perhaps a little dubious, but I consider it has more than just curiosity value; it is heartbreaking, well written, and fascinating. I will leave you, the reader, to separate the facts from fiction, or, to simply enjoy a fine piece of writing.

Those essays that discuss the works of authors he much admired are written with such passion and obvious love for the subject that I hope, like me, you find yourself carried along by his enthusiasm. One can also get a sense of the fiction he read as a boy shaping his own later career as a writer; the influences must have been very strong. Certainly in his correspondence to me, Porges would enthuse on the merits of such authors as H. H. Munro and H. Rider Haggard.

The bibliographic pieces, such as "Confessions of a Biblioneurotic," should provide amusement for those curious about such things and, even if not, one might see them as a stepping stone into the world, just for a little while, of the obsessed book-lover.

To wrap up this introduction, I would like to thank you for buying this book. I trust you'll find much to enjoy. The forthcoming second volume will gather together a selection of essays that Porges wrote on all manner of miscellaneous subjects. Less personal, for sure, but it's a wide-ranging pot pourri and absolutely fascinating!

For now, though, I leave you with this first volume. Arthur was as proud of these essays as he was of his short fiction, and after reading them I hope you will see why.

Richard Simms
West Sussex, England
January, 2021

Close Encounters
With the Fool-Killer

On Sunday, Dec. 23, 1888 this item appeared in *The New York Tribune*:

> Now and then Niagara has ably assisted the Fool-Killer by knocking out gentlemen who bid for fame by going over the Falls in a barrel.

This rather callous comment seems to be an early reference to a character of folklore born apparently in America. What comes to mind on hearing about an entity whose mission in life it is to terminate with prejudice—to use a modern phrase popular in espionage circles—those of us behaving rashly without regard for obvious consequences, is, "Man, talk about understaffing ... One executioner when legions would be overworked, overwhelmed, unable to kill more than a small fraction of the fools among us."

Then comes another thought: "Aha! Now I know why I escaped relatively unscathed after incredibly foolish behavior. The Fool-Killer had far too many targets, and most of us were spared."

And that reflection prompted me to look back on some close encounters of my own with the Fool-Killer.

An early instance occurred when I was about ten years old. My family had just moved to a rather decrepit neighborhood of Chicago, the Depression having driven us out of a better one with rents too high for my father's salary, which the phone company had cut.

I was unbelievably naive for my age, so when the boys of the community suggested a charming game of welcome I was delighted, since making friends in a new environment was always an ordeal.

The little game, they explained, was simple. They would scour the area for various souvenirs, usually from trash-cans, of interest to small fry like us: baby-carriage wheels, great for making scooters; abandoned magazines and books; bits of metal that might be sold to junkmen; boards, fine for hut-building or tree-houses—the list was endless. Happily, I agreed to wait at the designated spot—one where nosy, interfering, censorious adults couldn't spoil our sport—wearing a paper crown: a king, to whom my subjects, to prove their loyalty, would bring gifts. (How lucky for me that the Fool-Killer had his hands full among patrons of the stock market!)

It took the boys about an hour to return, heavily laden. At the last moment, they showed a trace of compassion, since instead of throwing their loot directly against my face and torso, they flung it mainly at my feet, splattering my long, brown stockings (in those days, one wore short-pants until puberty) with an odorous collection consisting of empty fish-cans, soiled paper wrappings, discarded medicine bottles, chicken bones and—worst of all—horse manure, easy to find what with milk carts and ice wagons still common.

Bewildered, shocked, I endured their raucous laughter and when they scattered I made my way home thoroughly sick at heart. Obviously, as is now clear, I took the affair too seriously, and later found several good friends among my tormentors. But then, you see, I was a booby, an innocent in a society growing ever more cynical. The Fool-Killer would have had every reason to terminate me, but I escaped. But for years I winced at the sight of a crown.

At sixteen, I again found myself at risk without then realizing it. It was a delicate matter, not acceptable to all as a lapse of judgment in these days of supposed return, however brief, to "traditional morality," which probably never existed in more than a minority among us. In any case, a PG rating may be in order here.

This next narrow escape from the Fool-Killer began when, as a high school junior, I lost my Waterman fountain pen, a much-cherished possession, since it was not only a birthday present but had my name on it in fancy gold letters.

It should be noted here that I was tall, quite strong, especially as to my arms, and not bad looking; but having been reared in an all-male family, presided over by a rather prudish father, I knew less about sex than about the agricultural products of Albania. My mother died when I was nine and my father never remarried. He might have done so, even with four sons and one arm, since he had a lifetime job with Illinois Bell, something not to be dismissed lightly in those terrible Depression days, and was a handsome, lovable man. But he was irrevocably romantically a one-woman male, and that was that. I might add that he never used language stronger than a rare "hell" or "damn," so that when in his seventies, I once heard him actually utter a four-letter word, one of the mildest, I was quite shocked.

So there I was, physically mature, emotionally and sexually a veritable fetus, facing—and too big a fool to know it!—a lovely seduction.

A call from the principal's office informed me, much to my relief, that the pen had been found and was being held for me, at a house just a few blocks from the school. I could pick it up after classes. Happily, I sought out the brick apartment building, rang the bell to the right flat and was admitted by a young, attractive woman, alone in the bright and well-kept parlor.

I immediately asked her for my pen, in a hurry to leave, but she acted, as I saw it then, very weirdly. Instead of giving it to me, she started to tell me how lonely and unhappy she was, illustrating her sad plight with little anecdotes about the husband who'd left her, the unfriendly neighbors who never entertained her in their homes and how much she needed to be loved.

Bewildered by this development, I again asked for my pen—had the Fool-Killer been near, he would have struck in a flash—and edged away when she put her hand on my arm, and then smoothed my hair.

Finally, unable to get her message across, she let me go and I almost ran, thinking I'd met up with an obviously deranged woman. I'd blown a perfect opportunity, one well appreciated in Europe, if not here, a chance to be initiated by a lovely, warm, intelligent older—she must have been all of thirty—lady. It wasn't until years later that I realized what I'd missed, which if taken gratefully would have saved me from much frustration and anguish.

In both these cases my sin was venial; I was guilty mainly of stupidity, not malice, greed or hubris. That was not true in those to come, where my pristine imbecility was indeed tainted by other faults.

Behold me next about to present my master's thesis research to a small audience at college. Seated in the front row is my sponsor, a brilliant young mathematician, kind but impatient with weaker intellects, a stern perfectionist on the writing and organizing of material. With the Depression still crushing the economy, he was able regardless to get the then unheard-of sum of fifty dollars an hour as a consultant to engineering firms on problems of cybernetics, in which he was a distinguished pioneer with a long list of publications in the most prestigious journals.

At twenty-two, I was glib and self-assured, never having had the slightest fear of addressing any number of people. I didn't realize, in my fatuous confidence, that it wouldn't do to present mathematical results in a casual, conversational way—not to these specialists in rigor.

So, inevitably, before I had spoken a dozen sentences I was in deep trouble and much to my consternation, my sponsor strode to the blackboard, shouldered me aside and made the presentation himself, outraged that I was botching his own elegant substructure of the research.

Burning with shame, I stood to one side for what seemed hours and later, when a few kindly professors implied I'd been treated with undue harshness, I could only mumble that I'd richly deserved all I'd got—which was true, and called for the attention of the Fool-Killer, busy this time in Nazi Germany, preparing for war and its ultimate destruction.

My next foolishness might have had far more serious consequences, and to others as well as me. The scene has shifted to Fort Sill, Okla., where as a newly minted second lieutenant in the field artillery I was immensely pleased with my status. That I, a child of immigrants, should actually be an officer, was unbelievable good fortune, a fact that had been hammered home a few weeks earlier by no less a person than actor Van Heflin, who as captain told a group of us that going from mere privates and noncoms—which we were at the start of Officer Candidate School—to lieutenants, was just like suddenly ascending from janitor to president of General Motors or whatever big firm. All actors tend to exaggerate.

That morning we were scheduled for firing practice with 105mm howitzers, so the battery made a ninety-minute hike to the target area. When the allowed number of rounds had been expended, the senior officers took off in a jeep, first ordering me to lead the men back to base. When they had gone, my second in command—thinking unenthusiastically of the tiring walk—suggested we could save a lot of time and effort by going ahead over some knolls instead of retracing the morning's route. Having no sense of direction myself, and forgetting that as the one in command, I, not

17

he, had all the responsibility for such a decision, I cheerfully assented and we set off, hoping to enjoy showers and chow early.

It wasn't until some 250mm rounds from huge howitzers—much bigger pieces than ours—exploded near us that I realized with horror that I'd led the hapless men right into an impact area. In moments, several excited, infuriated captains and colonels had descended upon us, thirsting for shavetail blood.

To make a sad story short, I ended up with a reprimand in my file, a mild punishment considering that I might have caused death and injury to the enlisted men in my charge. Only the fact that my orders had been oral, not written, and a little ambiguous saved me from a court-martial, which I fully merited. Had one of those monstrous shells detonated among, or even near, my group ... but I'd rather not think about that, even now, almost fifty years later. A fool I was, and lucky to escape Him.

And now the mad business of my first car, a saucy, new, red Volvo. Oddly, I didn't drive until into my forties and then after a few slapdash lessons from a friend. I got my license much too easily, which often happens in small towns; this one was Laguna Beach. And just a few weeks after qualifying, a less capable driver, I suspect, than even the legendary Mr. Toad, I set off for a new home in the San Francisco Bay Area—and taking the coast route, at that. Further, I'd greatly overloaded the Volvo with possessions: back seat and trunk were both full of heavy items, as was most of the front. The springs sagged and groaned under their burden; the frame almost scraped the road, yet I drove blithely along towering bluffs, often pushing seventy or more, inches from the edge. And having miraculously escaped a soggy demise in the Pacific, I compounded my idiocy by letting a clear, straight stretch of 101 near King City tempt me into finding out what the little car could do, flat out. What it could do, and even with that load, was a swaying ninety miles per hour plus.

Well, I survived, although having no more business going that fast in the circumstances than in taking over a Concorde in flight. And the Fool-Killer missed his big chance again.

Finally—not that age has put a full stop to my foolishness, but at least curtailed my verbosity about it—the affair of which I'm most ashamed, since it displayed not only stupidity but insensitivity and latent, perhaps subconscious racism.

I was seventeen and had just one semester to finish at high school when I was hit by scarlet fever, a fairly mild case, but no matter: it meant quarantine at the Municipal Contagious Disease Hospital. I lost the whole semester, not because of the scarlet fever, but because of what was called "dip throat"—that is, I tested positive for diphtheria, although free of the actual disease. That meant I could not be released until my cultures came up negative, free of the infection. For weeks I languished, hoping each day I'd make it out of there.

Finally, I heard whispers that a certain hospital attendant knew a way and could be induced to explain it. I dogged his footsteps for days (looking back now, I'm sure he wanted a sizeable tip, so to speak) and finally persuaded him to tell me the trick, which was to gargle with salt-water and expel some through the nose. Sure enough, after a few days, my culture was clear. What I didn't understand was that by using that gimmick, I was bypassing a vital safeguard for the community, since I'd almost certainly again be a carrier later.

That was bad enough, but when two young doctors—handsome, suave, self-assured and highly personable—questioned me, I betrayed without hesitation the man who had helped me. No doubt he was fired, a very serious thing with so many out of work. I didn't realize what I'd done; I was merely rejoicing in my escape and wanted to tell the world how clever my benefactor had been. It simply didn't dawn on me that the method was illegitimate, verboten, and dangerous.

During my long, wearisome stay of over ninety days, I became fond of the nurses, who did most of the work, with doctors rarely around. One of these, probably not an RN since most of the scut-work—floor-mopping, bedpans and enemas—fell to her, was black; "colored" was the word then. She was a warm, earthy, genial woman, who looked after my more intimate and embarrassing needs.

On the day I was scheduled to leave, I persuaded my father to bring a box of chocolates each for the nurses, but didn't include the black one. I don't know why and when she questioned me in a sad, resigned way, I don't recall my explanation, but it must have been lame and worthless. I could weep right now for the terrible, wanton hurt I gave her. If the Fool-Killer showed up, I'd not offer any resistance. But as Omar put it in words that can't be improved upon:

The Moving Finger writes: and, having writ,
Moves on; nor all your Piety nor Wit
Shall lure it back to cancel half a line,
Nor all your Tears wash out a word of it.

There have been other close encounters, but enough. Like Uncle Remus, "I knows lots more den I kin remember." To paraphrase a rueful comment of Mark Twain's, I've been a writer for thirty-five years and a fool for about seventy!

My only consolation at the moment is that most of you—yes, even you over there!—have had equally narrow escapes from the overworked Fool-Killer. Deny it if you can!

My First Bike

At the age of fifteen, unlike today's kids, I didn't yearn for a car, which would have been like hoping for a magic carpet. Few of my friends had any such an urge either. The zeitgeist was against the notion, even though a new Chevy could be had for a few hundred dollars. But it was the Great Depression, and even a ten-dollar purchase was not to be made lightly. There were, to be sure, a few eighteen-year-olds who could manage a used car, a jalopy, as the term went then, for fifty dollars, but for most of my peers, the Chicago streetcars, old, dirty, crowded, hot in summer, glacial in winter, sufficed for our commutes.

No, what I wanted, rather suddenly, with all my heart, was merely a bicycle. My two older brothers were quasi-experts, since they worked as special delivery messengers for the post office, and had to ride their battered two-wheelers even in the dreadful winters of below-zero temperatures, heavy snowfalls, and, worst of all, slick, dangerous sleet-coated streets.

My yearning was intensified when my two best friends, Marty and Ray, acquired bikes, which they used for all sorts of delightful excursions—to parks, the distant forest preserve, the baseball stadium, Wrigley Field, and the aquarium—in which I could participate only by riding on the luggage-carrier, which was uncomfortable and a bit humiliating.

After I had begged, pleaded, nagged, and made myself an intolerable nuisance, the family capitulated—up to a point—by studying the daily newspaper's want ads. For some reason, used bikes seemed to be scarce, so when an ad finally appeared, offering one—in fine condition—for only five dollars, I was very excited, and persuaded my oldest brother to go some eight miles with me to inspect the item. He was the expert, and also as second in command to my father, authorized to spend the fairly modest sum if satisfied of a fair buy.

So off we went, on the streetcar, of course, and in the garage of a pleasant, genial man found the bicycle in question. It was huge, to begin with, having, I believe, not the customary twenty-one inch wheels of the day, but thirty-inch giants. As to brand or model, it was a Columbia, a name vaguely familiar, but not very. In truth, it was an antique, almost a museum piece; no Columbias had been made for decades, probably. But I was consumed with my desire to own a bike, any old bike, and although my brother, Leonard, had some doubts, he gave in to my pleas and paid the five dollars. Foolishly, on both our parts, we didn't even ride the thing, but just accepted the seller's word that it was in top condition, and a great bargain.

Fired with enthusiasm, I was ready to ride it back the full eight miles, with Leonard following on the streetcar, but he thought it would be better to stash it on the back platform, lest so long a trip for a novice—I'd only been riding a few days, and weirdly, as you'll see—be too tricky, even dangerous.

So we hauled it aboard, amid many jeers by people who thought it crazy to pay fare for a vehicle that should have been its own, and my, free transportation.

At last, however, when we left the streetcar four blocks from home, as near as it came to our apartment, I had my chance to ride it. I had gone only a few hundred feet when I became aware that something was not right with the gearing; the bike had a catch, a sort of hiccup, in the transmission, which made the pedaling unpleasantly arduous. In fact, even after four blocks, I was weary, and shuddered at the narrow escape I'd had in avoiding the full eight-mile trip.

Well, I had made my bed, and so said little about the bike's serious disability; but when I rode with my two friends, I must have used at least twice the energy for half the speed, although the oversized wheels gave me some advantage regardless.

I come now to the unique peculiarity of my style. Despite the best efforts of my brothers, I had been unable to mount a bike the normal way. My legs were too short for a straddle when the machine was stationary, and swinging aboard after giving it a push, totally beyond me, so I would lean the bike against a fence, say, or post, mount it, and then push off. That was bizarre enough, but far worse was the matter of dismounting. Unless I pulled up and stopped near some support, my only way of ending the ride was to stop and then fall over, bike and all.

That routine led to one particularly distressing event. Coming up on the sidewalk one morning on a visit to the library, I somehow bungled my stop along the wall, and took an unusually bad fall, a bit more strenuous than my usual dismounting-by-collapse. Unfortunately, a little girl had just emerged from the library, and my descending handlebars missed her by only inches. Her father, just behind her in the entrance, charged out, practically frothing. He swore at me, and viciously kicked at the bike, having no regard whatever for its age and disability. I was lucky to escape in a shower of vituperation without injury.

On hearing of this incident, my two friends decided it was past time to reform me; this business of needing a fence to get on or off was patently unacceptable. I still couldn't straddle the high-saddled machine, so they took a different tack, a method something like the one in cowboy movies, where Tom Mix or somebody would run alongside a horse and scramble aboard with a well-timed hop and skip. Miraculously, their approach worked at once. I could wheel the bike along with one foot on a pedal, and as it built up speed, swing onto the seat. Suddenly, I was liberated, free of posts, fences, bruises, and fleering laughter from other kids.

Confessions of a Sports Klutz

My participation in sports when I was a boy—as an adult, I soon lost interest, never to regain it—was much like the curate's famous breakfast egg: good in spots. In short, I was a quirky, unpredictable performer, capable of occasionally surprising and shocking a much better trained athlete, but always without even a trace of good form, a klutzy nuisance to traditional players.

Unlike most kids, I didn't start with baseball, football or basketball, but the rather wimpy game of—as it was called then—ping-pong, later given the more appealing, less sissy, name of table tennis. In the depths of the Great Depression, my family, a motherless one, would not have dreamed of buying a regulation table and equipment; money was hard to come by; and in our smallish apartment, housing a father and four sons, there wasn't room for it, either.

So what we did acquire was a pair of cheap, wooden paddles, a flimsy green net and two clamps with which it could be fastened to an ordinary rectangular dining table, which we did have. It was, however, only about two-thirds as long as the real one used by pros. As a consequence, my brother Irwin and I became quite good at playing the game under unique restrictions. We had to keep the lively ball within very narrow bounds, but, even worse, were unable to use the basic ploy of rapidly backing up in order to soften and return a hard drive by one's opponent. At short range, such a fast ball got past us too quickly to counter most of the time.

On the other hand, for obvious reasons, we were almost unbeatable on our own turf. When a friend of the family's, a good player who had won several local tournaments, dropped in and was suckered into a game, his smugness soon vanished. What with our penholder grips, then becoming obsolete—the pros held their paddles exactly like tennis rackets—and our heavy, unbalanced, wooden paddles, added to the serious handicap of a short table, he was massacred.

Weak, generally, as the penholder grip was, compared to the new one that was favored by experts, it was more suitable to a murderous backhand, which Irwin and I had mastered. One shot after another, driven by sweeping backhand strokes, bounced past our frustrated friend, who could have whipped either of us easily on a regulation table and using paddles covered with pebbled rubber.

Later, of course, we moved on to more realistic conditions, playing often at a pool hall, which rented tables for twenty-five cents an hour. It was there that we became moderately good at the game, but never first, or even second, class. In fact, any delusions we had about being qualified were quickly demolished, first, by the family friend, Lou, who rarely allowed us even ten points of the twenty-one needed to win a game. He was followed by a whole galaxy of men, women and children who left Irwin and me for dead every time we showed up to challenge them.

There were some fascinating oddballs among our antagonists. One was Max, a melancholy, saturnine Russian, who later became a national contender, winner of many tournaments. I beat him only once, when he was broodingly absent-minded, not really caring about the game, but only the free practice—I paid the two bits for the rental equipment. He didn't even bother to take his special racket out of its velvet pouch, but used house paddles, battered and peeling rubber.

Then there was Sugarman, well named by fate or synchronicity or something. He was casual, careless, even inept—until one was tricked into a bet. Then, coldly, calmly, with a granite countenance, he became unbeatable. I guess you could call him a sort of ringer, a ping-pong version of Minnesota Fats in *The Hustler*. I foolishly tried many times, but never won a bet with him. "Sugar," as all called him, was not interested in tournaments; not for him a cheap cup thinly plated with silver; he wanted hard cash or nothing. Once, after being beaten by him again, the loser remarked sourly that if somebody would make a ten-dollar wager with Sugar, he'd undoubtedly take on, and whip, the world champion ... at that time a spectacularly gifted young Chinese.

One amazing player was barely out of childhood; he must have been no older than ten. He was short, plump and solemn. "Chubby," as he was called, was quite good from the start; few could defeat him; but he quickly became a real master, later to win many major contests. His forte was an impregnable defense. Imperturbably that apple-cheeked kid would return anything, no matter how hard-driven; none of us could get through him.

I played the game on and off for several years, but won only one prize, or rather, half of one: a small chintzy trophy for a victory, with Lou, in doubles. I don't know what happened to it; the tarnished metal cup vanished decades ago.

About the time my interest in ping-pong began to flag, there was a sudden influx of Oriental whizzes. They were young, unbelievably agile, innovative, versatile and fiercely dedicated to the game. They were entirely out of our class; our best players went down before them like spring wheat at harvest time. In fact, they dominated the sport for years. But I was no longer involved.

It was natural progression, I suppose, from table tennis to the real sport, played with full-sized rackets on a grass or clay court. And here again, I began with a cheap, limply strung racket and no instruction whatever. My only talent, if it could be so called, was that of being fast on my feet. I could cover the court wonderfully, but had no strokes to profit from that gift. For example, I could never master a simple drive, yet, for some reason, had a very strong backhand. It's as if one could ride a motorcycle but not a tricycle.

And yet, oddly, I occasionally surprised very capable players who had all the standard traditional strokes down pat. It wasn't the powerful backhand, but a variety of cuts and chops I'd developed, including one zany stroke, which I thought I'd invented, but learned later was called a "renshaw." Using such devices, I could deliver a ball that looked easy, but would suddenly swerve, bounce crookedly, or even reverse on hitting the ground.

I can recall, however, only one memorable triumph, a touch of glory, which still tickles me a little after about fifty-five years. I rashly entered a tournament scheduled at River Park in Chicago. By chance, my first game was against the top seed, a rather smug, supercilious young socialite, whose friends laughingly predicted my quick and total defeat. A bit resentful—and with nothing to lose—I unleashed all my quirky cuts and slices, so confusing and frustrating my opponent that even his excellent drives failed.

I was also helped by my equally bizarre serve. I was never able to attain the ordinary kind. I would toss the ball up and strike it manfully—right over the fence. I simply couldn't manage the topspin or whatever to make the ball land anywhere near the opposite half of the court. Yet other boys, far shorter than I—I was almost six feet tall, with strong arms—had no trouble. So, having no alternative, I again resorted to a slow but weirdly spinning ball. It would sail over the net, in a leisurely float, and land. And when my opponent was ready to give it a mighty smash, it would zip to one side or stop almost dead without even bouncing.

As a result, I had several aces and actually took the first set. Of course, it couldn't last. My opponent was too well trained and capable not to dredge up the right counter-strokes, and easily won the next two sets to end the match. But at least the snickering at me stopped.

As to baseball, there is precious little to tell and even less to brag about. When my brothers and I helped make up a bungling nine on some empty lot for a game of softball, I was a fair hitter, couldn't pitch at all, was hopeless as an infielder, being unable to catch grounders, which hopped almost insolently over my hands, and erratic in the outfield.

My sole triumph occurred in high school. The gym teacher, an ex-military man, drilled us a lot—his sharp "Hup! Hup!" sounded to my bored ears like the beats of a motorboat—and when feeling lazy, sent us out to play softball. One day, when I was covering—to flatter myself—center field, a husky lad hit a tremendous fly, one of the longest any of us had ever seen. Fleet of foot, I raced toward the fence, got under the ball and—never dreaming of actually touching it—held out my hands. Wonder of wonders! I seized the ball and somehow retained it. My teammates cheered, since I had never impressed them before, but they were undoubtedly less surprised than I was. Never again did I make a catch even half that remarkable, but went on dropping most balls that descended upon me.

I will also confess—I'm ashamed of such infantile passion now—that I was for a few years a rabid fan of the Chicago Cubs, a pathetic bunch of losers even then—although the local sports announcer, Hal Totten, bent over backwards to favor them in his radio broadcasts. I was so hyped up about the team, in fact, that on one occasion when the veteran Riggs Stephenson, an aging titan rarely used, was brought in as pinch-hitter (there were no "pinch-batters" then) in an almost hopeless attempt to save the day, and hit a mighty double, I immediately scribbled that miracle down in a notebook, along with a fervent, "Lest we forget!" and the date.

When it comes to football, my slate is almost blank. I couldn't throw even a short pass that didn't wobble crazily in flight like a mortally wounded, overweight duck. Most of my peers could have hurled the whole pig more effectively. Nor could I punt. Neither my toe nor my instep succeeded in making solid contact with the ball.

Worse, I wasn't sure then (and still am not) which part of my foot was supposed to do the job. As a result, the ball would fly weakly to one side, then drop as if brought down by a missile. Yet here again is the typically odd pattern; I had a rather good dropkick, which puzzled my companions, who knew, rightfully, that punting ought to be easy and dropkicking tricky. Well, that's the football story, and nary one moment of glory to recall.

And now, finally, a sport, game, child-play, whatever, that's unique and seems to have sunk without a trace, since I've never heard of its being played after my own time and place. We called it Horse and Rider, and it consisted of having a young kid climb on the back of an older, bigger one, locking his legs around the "steed's" neck. Then two such combos would go at each other, with riders striving mightily either to pull the little kid off the big one or topple both. As you see, it was roughly like a medieval joust between two knights. In this case, my glory lasted a bit longer; I was local champ for a week or two.

I bowled only once, racking up all of forty points and irking the lane's owner, who winced as my inept delivery threatened to dent the hardwood. And I was totally baffled by the method of scoring. 'Nuf said!

Well, today it's all water over an ancient dam. For the last fifty-odd years, sports have meant nothing to me; in fact, my interest would have to triple to approach apathy, and I'm ever more bemused by the passions they arouse in the American public. But then, I'm the odd man out. Maybe I'd still like sports if the Olympic Games included Horse and Rider … nah, that's silly!

A Short and
Inglorious Work Resume

My lifetime job experience, aside from teaching, rather a special case, with ivory-tower implications, was short, inglorious, and a bit bizarre. It began in 1932 when I was seventeen, and the Great Depression had the world by the throat. There should have been a similar depression of the national spirit, suggestive of the Chinese proverb, "If grief, like fire, but gave forth smoke, ever it would be night on Earth," yet, oddly, that was not so for much of the country. Instead, there was a we're-all-in-this-together feeling that seemed to buoy people up and make them want to share what little they had.

I had a cousin who was a year younger than I, but whose family was considerably worse off, thanks to a spendthrift father and feckless mother. They were barely making it, reminding my own more stable dad of the fellow who was always a dollar short, an hour late, and headed in the wrong direction.

My cousin, Ira, was working every weekend at a big downtown department store in Chicago, where we lived then. One night, when as often happened—deliberately, we suspected, since food was in short supply at his home—he was having dinner with us, Ira suggested that by using his influence, he could get me on the store's payroll for a big upcoming sale in the shoe department. The pay was little enough, about forty cents an hour, but could be useful to my hard-pressed family. After all, a loaf of bread was a dime, and round steak about thirty cents a pound, so one could feed several people on an hour's take.

At that time in Chicago, the two prestige department stores were Carson, Pirie, Scott & Company, and Marshall Field's. Both had the pick of part-time labor—and any other kind, in fact, jobs being so scarce—so Ira was lucky to find work at the third place, a rather schlock operation, almost a discount house, which treated its employees more like slaves than hired help. It catered to the poorest stratum of consumers, the kind that were not welcome at the other stores. Thanks to Ira, I was hired one Saturday for a huge shoe sale.

Now, I had never worked a day in my life, except for certain tasks in a motherless home, like shopping, cooking, and dishwashing. I knew nothing about the business world, and even less about shoes, being unfamiliar even with the basic sizes. Yet, without any training, I suddenly found myself in a mad rush of customers as the doors opened on the sale at eight a.m.

I had been given an order book and a pencil, and was wearing a name-tag to distinguish me from the frantic buyers. There was little enough status in the job for even the haggard veterans, so my own standing was well under zero to all concerned, who regarded me, reasonably enough, I had to concede, as more of an obstacle, something annoying underfoot, than a colleague.

To make matters worse, it was one of those dreadfully hot, humid summer days so common in Chicago; and in minutes I was drenched, rumpled, and wild-eyed. We had to wear jackets and ties, very oppressive in such weather, but mandated by the store's brass. Those were far more formal times than now; a sport shirt, loafers, or shaggy hair meant no job, period.

That was a bad enough start, but I soon made two embarrassing errors as well. The shoes were tied together in pairs by bits of twine. Since nobody instructed me otherwise, and I was too distraught to see the obvious, I somehow assumed shoes couldn't be tried on unless separated. So behold me clawing, pulling, dripping as I attempted to break the tough twine before servicing an impatient customer. I had pulled a number apart, sometimes ruining the cheap material, when a compassionate customer, a motherly woman, suggested, in a gentle voice, that maybe I wasn't supposed to do that, that it wasn't really necessary, was it? My blush must have added ten degrees to the already unbearable temperature. But from then on, I slipped a shoe on one foot with the other still attached—and it worked perfectly. But no doubt I'd damaged enough leather to make me a liability to the store; in short, they surely lost money on me. I should have solicited fees from the other two stores as their agent, busily sabotaging the competition.

My next blunder was even more stupid. In a state of near-hysteria by then—the day was wearing on, quickly, I admit, so busy was I—and looking for the next customer, I cornered a young woman, babbling, "Can I help you?" She glared at me, and I repeated the query.

"You jerk!" she snarled, shoving me away. "Don't you see my tag?" She was, I then realized—too late—a fellow wage-slave, just as wilted, far better at the job, and panting to disembowel me as an intolerable pest adding to her misery. I slunk away.

When the store closed at ten p.m., I had racked up forty dollars in sales, about a quarter of what the experienced help, including Ira, had taken in. No doubt any profit I'd brought the store was insufficient to pay for merchandise I'd ruined.

When I got home, tired, soaked, and very hyper, my father took one look and decided immediately I was not cut out to be a sales clerk, and probably not qualified for anything but office work. He was surely right; never again did I try to sell anything.

My second non-teaching job came eleven years later; it was non-profit, tricky, and one for which I had no background whatever. Nor did I have any choice about accepting it, since I was a brand new second lieutenant, and the Army made me an offer I could not refuse!

My total ignorance was no excuse; it has always been a military axiom that if a general told anybody of lower rank to do something, even if it called for making a stick with only one end, he did it, or else. In my case, the Army was right; I learned fast, and coped.

In a way, I was partly to blame. Some months earlier, when the new officers' club was being built, I sneered at plans for a semicircular bar, urging instead one shaped like half an ellipse. Asked how that could be done, I promptly used a basic construction from analytic geometry, which needed only two big nails, some string, and a bit of chalk. Proudly I drew the outline on the floor, and rather to my surprise, the brass bought it, and the bar was built to that configuration.

I was pleased until—now to the point—the same powers-that-be appointed me Mess Officer. There was further irony in that, since I was responsible for buying liquor, managing the bar, even to being bartender at times, and keeping the books, all terra incognita to me.

As noted, I did master the record-keeping, which also included pestering those officers who never paid their bills on time, screwing up my books.

On the plus side, I had access to the kitchen, was deferred to by the cooks, and when the other men had to eat fish on Friday—most didn't like it—I would saunter out of the pantry with big hunks of baloney. No doubt my fellow soldiers would have enjoyed strangling me on the spot. But did any officer volunteer for my job? As Mark Twain would say, I should smile! Why fish was served at all, I never knew for sure. Protestants hinted at Roman Catholic influence (many high-ranking officers were Irish); others pointed out that, in civilian life, meat was rationed, and the military didn't like to flaunt its freedom from such controls.

My next, and actually last, job, unless I start hunting for one again—not so wildly improbable if prices keep going up!—was also by courtesy of the Army, and—need I say it?—found me completely ignorant of the basics. The same mysterious rankers—or their clones— apparently, now decreed I was to be battalion adjutant, the hapless soul in charge of plans and training. As a first lieutenant now, they thought I was qualified; if not, too bad; I'd have to learn, and fast.

I must admit the Army had succeeded in making me think I could indeed do anything. Some weeks before I'd been ordered to conduct a Formal Guard Mount, an awesome drill with more pitfalls than a Vietnam battlefield. Luckily, an old sergeant had warned me about the worst mistakes, citing cases of junior officers who forgot some vital step, leaving the men "At ease," when they should have been "At attention," or facing the right instead of left, so I got through it, miraculously, without a single blunder, although my voice quavered more than once. A very complicated business, nothing like the simple close-order drill I knew well.

As Mess Officer, I still had to carry out my other, more military duties, chiefly those of executive of a 105mm howitzer battery. But being an adjutant is a full-time job, in spades. I needed most of the day, and often part of the night, just to assemble the giant crossword puzzle that was the core—and bane—of my work. It was, actually, the weekly training schedule, and very tricky. Every activity was allotted so many hours, and had to fit in with all the others. But, in addition, there were restrictions; for example, exercise, route-marches, obstacle course runs, and similar vigorous activities could not be set late in the day, but only early in the morning, when the men were fresh and the air cool.

There had to be alternatives, too. If the weather was very bad, with rain or wind, target practice was out, so I'd better have a training film or lecture lined up.

That called for considerable ingenuity, and at first I sweated, swore, and groaned over the infuriating chart, only to have the major point out some flaw, which, often as not, meant starting again from scratch—the hateful blank page.

But, finally, as with all learning, the difficult became easy, routine, so that I wondered why it had taken me so long to master something really simple. And I understood, for the first time, what the major had meant, when on my first day as adjutant, he'd pulled open the desk drawer to show a number of colored glass spheres.

"What are those for?" I inquired, a perfect straight man.

He smiled, not without a touch of malice, although a kindly old retread, and said, "Oh, those are all the marbles previous adjutants lost trying to do the job."

As it happened, his little ambush was a total flop; I was simply not familiar with the phrase, apparently not current in Chicago. Or maybe it was one of those "Old" (or "Regular") Army sayings new to me, so it wasn't until I'd questioned him that I got the point. In any case, he—and my father—had it exactly right: this sort of work was not for me, and once free to choose again, I stuck to teaching math!

Grocery Shopping
—The Way it Was

Very few shoppers today would recognize the once familiar phrases "soup greens" and "soup bone," but there was a time, during the Great Depression of 1932 when mom-and-pop stores struggled desperately for survival, and each customer was cherished, even coddled. Supermarkets were almost unknown. Oh, there was The Great Atlantic and Pacific Tea Company, the famous A&P chain, and a then-new one with the eyebrow raising name of Piggly Wiggly, but neither firm had an outlet in or near my community. We had to settle for a variety of small stores concentrated in Chicago's many business districts.

It was also a time of ethnicity and great individuality. There were shops with signs reading Zaretsky's Grocery, Himmelblau's German Bakery, Breger's Meats, O'Doul Hardware and Luigi Bulloni: Fresh Fish, the latter a dark, tiny store. Poor Luigi, daily some impudent kid would ask him when he'd give up on herring and sell—what else?—baloney! His wife, improbably a red-haired Irish woman, was rumored to have once bounced a large flounder off the head of a too-persistent smart aleck. And aside from actual shops, there were many sidewalk vendors, including bearded, black-capped, Orthodox Jews, who sold freshly ground, red-dyed, incredibly hot horseradish.

But getting back to my opening phrases. If you asked a clerk in Alpha Beta today for soup greens or a nice bone, you'd get at best a blank stare. But during the Depression, when it was hard to sell even prime vegetables and steak, every merchant took it for granted that he must cheerfully hand out, even to people buying two bits' worth of anything, a large handful of vegetables good for making soup, but not, presumably, saleable on its own. The handout might include parsley, wilted carrots, celery tops, small, green-spotted potatoes, deteriorating onions and anything else no longer fresh and desirable. Similarly, at the butcher's, if you bought some ground meat at fifteen cents a pound or whatever, you had every right to obtain for free a large bone, one that might even have a few ounces of flesh still on it. It was called a soup bone and, in fact, was so used.

In a way, the ritual at both stores relates to a delightful folk story used by, among others, the great poet William Butler Yeats, who wrote a one-act play, a minor masterpiece, on the theme, *The Pot of Broth*.

The fable usually begins with a tramp appearing at some farmer's house and declaring he has a magic nail from which one can actually make a thick, rich, nutritious soup. All that's needed is good, pure water and a large pot.

This story invariably hypnotized the farmer or, even better, if he was busy in the lower forty, his bored wife, enchanted by the charming, scoundrelly stranger with his magic nail and roving, impudent eye. Quickly, eager to watch the amazing bit of metal in action, she provides a large cauldron full of well-water. As the liquid heats up, nearing a boil, with the shiny nail visible at the bottom of the pot, the visitor remarks casually that tasty as such a soup is, it's bound to be even better if one adds a carrot or two, and perhaps a small onion. Immediately the housewife procures these supplements, and as the stranger rambles on, quietly stirring the soup, he mentions that salt and pepper also help, making for a superb broth, although—he repeatedly stresses—the wonderful nail alone does a great job.

Well, the point of this ancient scam is clear: the dupe, unwittingly, supplies all the vital ingredients, but is convinced the nail has supernatural valuable qualities, and is delighted to be able to buy it—only because the tramp is hard up—for a modest few shillings—or greenbacks—or, as in the case with Hans Christian Andersen's odd, witty variant, *Soup From a Sausage Peg*, marriage to a reigning king who wants the secret.

As to making the rounds daily in order to feed a family, that chore fell mainly to my kid brother, because my father and two older brothers had jobs. Our mother had died years before, and so we five males were on our own. I had only high school to cope with, getting out by noon, and so became the family cook. I was chiefly self-taught at the job, and could turn out reasonably good roasts, stews and broiled meats. We were then, like much of the country, meat and potato-eaters; salads were rare among the common folks, and chicken tended to be a holiday treat. Needless to say, although porterhouse and sirloin steaks were dirt-cheap by today's standards, wages were low and most people settled for cheaper cuts. The meat was often tough, gristly and tasteless.

Once, my imagination over-busy, I attempted to overcome that problem by using a spice-overkill: I cut dozens of little slits in the dreadful chunk of meat and inserted a clove of garlic in each. The result could have been smelled in the Chicago suburbs, but nobody could deny the roast had flavor! My family, good natured and tolerant, made only a few low-key objections, and I abandoned that ploy for good.

I never tried to do much with chicken and for, to me, good and sufficient reasons. There was no place to buy separately packaged parts, the neatly prepared drumsticks, breasts or wings of today.

Most homemakers not only settled for the whole fowl—chicken, duck or turkey—but had to clean it, and the insides of a cold-storage bird seemed appallingly messy to a kid like me. In fact, I recall watching, with a kind of sick fascination, how my mother or aunt would plunge their hands into the tangled innards while preparing a hen for the pot.

Similarly, I backed away from fish, the smell of which revolted me. I know better now, but there is some evidence that strong flavors bother children far more than adults. Most of us, once grown up, come to enjoy pungent spices and even the ripest of cheeses.

One of the few useful secrets about cooking that I did learn pertained to production of a good stew. I finally figured out that my pale, unappetizing looking dish, while tasting fairly good, lacked the proper color more than anything else. At last the right solution dawned on me: I merely had to brown the meat in some bacon-grease before stewing it. After that, the appearance was beyond criticism and, for some reason, even made the meat taste better.

The merchants of those long ago days, although obviously trying to please their customers—it was, after all, a life-and-death concern, since there were many stores that failed—still did not abandon their individual temperaments. One of them, a delicatessen owner with the peculiar name of Batt, never hesitated to argue politics and economics with my father, and each man had his own solution on how to end the Depression. A portly man, red-faced, irritable and voluble, Batt would often end up with the exasperated roar, "Let me 'splain you sometin'!" and proceed to enlighten my father, who, though he had a strong, vibrant voice himself, was unable to outshout his adversary.

Another unique merchant was the butcher, whose shop bore a large sign: Breger's Meats Is A Family Treat. My kid brother, like me a bit of a grammatical snob, winced on reading this and tried to make Breger replace "is" with "are," or to change "Meats" to the correct singular case, but the butcher was not about to take dictation from kids, and the sign stayed.

My stint as a cook went on for years, and on several occasions I surprised and delighted relations by my ability to produce a roast with suitable side dishes without spending a lot of time in the kitchen. I would engage in much casual conversation with them, checking the stove only occasionally, yet, promptly at six, the juicy roast, accompanied by beautifully browned potatoes, would be smoking on the table. Even for a trained cook, they implied, that was an amazing performance; for a boy like me, a miracle.

Once, years earlier, my younger brother and I, eager to give the family a real treat, determined to do something different. Instead of buying a pie or cake, we'd make a dessert on our own. As it happened, the house boasted only one cookbook, *The White House Cookbook*, a fat volume never intended for a Depression or poor people; it was definitely for rich gourmets. The only recipe we found that seemed remotely affordable and practicable was a concoction called—so help me—A Cheap Cream Cake. Well, we actually made the thing, and aside from a messy kitchen, full of pots, pans, mixing bowls and spills, it was edible; our elders ate it without cringing and with a minimum of criticism.

About that time one of my brothers, stuck with cooking for a day, invented a new dish: veal chops simmered in milk. It wasn't as bad as it sounds, and, in fact, we ate it on and off for years. Of course, the idea horrified our neighbors upstairs when they heard about it. They were Orthodox Jews and kept a kosher house. It was not only verboten to eat milk and meat together, but even to use the same plates, so the notion of stewing veal in milk was beyond the pale. They had a right to criticize, because the mother was a superb cook. In her kitchen I tasted two dishes that were simply incomparable, unique; nowhere else have I ever enjoyed them. The first was potatoes cooked very slowly somehow for twenty-four hours at a low heat. They came out soft, brown, and indescribably delicious.

She called them "chont" ("tschundt?")—I never saw the name in print, so must rely on that oral version. Her other little miracle was a kind of roll with a cottage cheese filling, perhaps a variant of the blintz, familiar to readers of Damon Runyon's stories about his oddball characters lunching at Mindy's. Nothing I've eaten since had so delicate a flavor, so subtly tasty a dough. She measured nothing; it was just a dab of this or that plus pure genius or instinct. Years later I tried to bake some of these, but lacked her unique gift. (Mrs. Weinberg called these "floddin.")

Inevitably, our family broke up. My two older brothers married, and were concerned only with their own homes; my kid brother went off to college and later became a teacher; I stayed with my father for a time while starting my own career in the classroom first, and then the Army. But long after the Depression we still reminisced about those bittersweet days when Walter, my younger brother, who loathed shopping and resented having to make the rounds of so many places each afternoon, tried very hard to cover all the bases on a single foray through the business section of the community, and so often staggered home lugging a huge bag that would have thrown out Paul Bunyan's back. We called him, much to his chagrin, "One-Trip Mefoofsky," after an amusing character invented by columnist Walter Winchell and used occasionally as a foil by him.

Today, in the vast, gleaming aisles of Nob Hill or whatever supermarket, when I see fancy vegetables selling at astronomical prices, and few meats under two dollars a pound, I think wistfully about soup greens and huge, fleshy, marrow-filled beef bones, both free for the asking in the world of 1932. *Sic transit gloria mundi.*

But, on the other hand, I must admit there were times, during my novitiate as a conscripted chef, when I empathized with the hapless soldier in Henri Barbusse's powerful 1916 antiwar novel, *Under Fire*. Delegated to carry rations from the rear to the gaunt, exhausted frontline troops, he would have the big marmites of reeking, congealed, nameless messes set down near the hungry men and try to scuttle away before being asked angrily, "What are they giving us today?" But if cornered, he had worked out a clever reply. He would merely shrug, roll his eyes upwards, disclaiming all responsibility for what the cooks had wrought, point to the food and say, "It's there!"

I never resorted to that particular evasion, but occasionally, when I'd turned out something particularly deplorable, I longed to find that good (and weasel-worded) a reply.

The Fruit That Got Away

As a youth during the Great Depression of the Thirties, I seldom had a chance to eat out, since money was hard to come by, and restaurant food, while absurdly cheap compared to what we're paying, unhappily, today, cost substantially more than that prepared at home.

But when I did indulge, by myself, with a date, or my family, and the waitress was amiable—being pretty didn't hurt!—I would occasionally tease her by asking for durian cream pie. Usually, she would blink and do a double take, then recite the standard list of chocolate, banana, coconut, and berry. Some of these often turned out not to be the real thing, but meringue, a gluey concoction I detested.

What was I looking for, anyway? Well, I certainly didn't expect to find any, not here in the United States, and, as far as I knew, not even in Asia. It was just a family joke, but the durian fruit itself is very real and remarkable. Some years earlier, I had read a most entertaining book about trapping wild animals on the Malay peninsula; it was by a man named Mayer, and along with many exciting accounts of his capturing tigers and other valuable beasts for zoos all over the world, he described in fascinating detail daily life among the native peoples.

One of his minor digressions, which much intrigued me, was his report on the durian tree, which bore a bizarre fruit, covered with formidable spikes over a hard shell. The fruit was so delicious that Malays would actually camp under the tree for days, waiting for a ripe one to drop. Even wild beasts, Mayer asserted, rushed in from miles around when that happened. Since not even the keenest of ears could possibly hear the faint thump as a durian plunked down on soft, matted undergrowth, it had to be something else that alerted them, and indeed it was; nobody could miss it—the smell!

This delectable fruit, in fact, has a truly horrible odor, which has been likened to cream cheese, strong onion, and much worse, like Limburger and even rotten meat. On the other hand, the pulp is a superb dish, said to taste like almond-butter-custard.

The tree itself grows to eighty or ninety feet, and is almost unclimbable, so that only by waiting for a ripe specimen to fall can anybody hope to indulge—after eluding or fighting off tigers, wild pigs, and scads of other greedy fauna.

A Lady Brassey, traveling with her husband, Thomas, a British Earl, on their ship, *Sunbeam*, late in the nineteenth century, wrote:

... we tried a durian, the fruit of the East ... and having got over the first horror of the onion-like odor we found it by no means bad.

She was obviously harder to please than most travelers, who thought it to be just about the most wonderful fruit on the face of the Earth. There were, in 1936 in Chicago, almost no exotic fruits of any kind. We ate, when lucky, apples—there was a splendid variety, no longer easily found, if at all, but the best I've ever eaten: russet— bananas, oranges, and, very rarely, fresh pineapple. So my interest in the durian, aroused by Mayer's witty account, is understandable.

Of course, I've never found any durian cream pie, although, I'm told, the fruit itself is sometimes available in specialty gourmet shops. And I now have to shun all such fatty desserts, lest my caring GP excommunicate me, but I will confess that if some local baker one day features fresh durian cream pie at, say, five dollars, I'd be tempted to eat a tiny, ten degree wedge!

Some Encounters
With the Written Word

I don't know very much about how young children relate to the written word these days, although they are no doubt quite familiar with "Zap!" and "Wow!" from the Saturday morning cartoon shows on TV.

On the other hand, we're told that those who watch *Sesame Street*, even mere toddlers, soon recognize both letters and numbers, and can joyously squeak out their names.

As a struggling young reader myself, long ago when there was no TV, I had a number of amusing encounters with written words. One of the first I can recall was "misled." Never having heard it pronounced, or, perhaps, not recognizing it when spoken, I thought of it mentally as "mizzled." I had a pretty good idea of what it meant but didn't realize it was actually a sort of compound word, made up of "mis" and "led." Surely a person who was mizzled was confused, baffled and frustrated. It sounded exactly right so interpreted, and even now I almost prefer that version.

Somewhat later my mistake was indeed one of pronunciation, not comprehension, a less excusable case than that of "misled." My father had arrived in this country about 1890 speaking no English, and, as a youth, should not have learned it quite as easily as a child can learn a new language. But thanks to the New York schools and his own intelligence, he rapidly became not only literate but an avid reader.

He loved Westerns, especially those of Clarence E. Mulford, who created "Hopalong Cassidy." Dad liked "Hoppy" well enough, but much preferred another character, one "Mesquite Jenkins," who was more cold, detached and lethal. He also read and enjoyed the "Red Clark" series of Gordon Young about a young, wiry, naive do-gooder, very fast with a gun, who went about confounding villains and saving young maidens.

Inevitably I dipped into the same books and was incautious enough one day at dinner to refer casually to a "dee-pyooty" sheriff, which brought gales of derisive laughter from my elders at the table.

There were other words in my life that presented no problems of pronunciation or comprehension but had near-talismanic powers for me and my younger brother, Walter. One such was a chemical name we ran across—where or how I can no longer even guess. It was not something found everywhere. The word in question was "diorthopyrocatechinol," which rolls off the tongue wonderfully well, like an incantation. How we loved to use it on every occasion! We would solemnly tell our schoolmates that at breakfast we had a whole glassful of fresh, sweet diorthopyrocatechinol, with our toast. We never tired of such tricks, even if they did.

I even used the word in a story I wrote decades later, which appeared in a men's magazine. I had the subject of the story, a fellow very mentally disturbed who constantly claimed great discoveries in many fields, boast that he had found a complete, perfect cancer-cure. It was—you guessed it—a simple, overlooked chemical, called diorthopyrocatechinol. (I still enjoy saying it as I write it!)

There were, too, many baffling foreign names in the books Walter and I read. What we did to a villain in the "Frank Merriwell" series by Burt L. Standish, one Porfias del Norte, I cringe to recall.

It would send any Hispanic into hysterics. We may have thought of him as that perfidious guy, Norton.

Yet, a bit paradoxically, when an older brother was taking French in high school, Walter and I picked his brains enough to invent a nice phrase of greeting: *"Qu'est-ce que le mot, oiseau?"* (What's the word, bird?)

In that far off time of my youth, with the huge late nineteenth-century wave of immigration still having its effects, there were a number of foreign language papers in Chicago, but the only one I knew about was the *Abend-Post*, a German one. I didn't know that its title meant "Evening Mail" and couldn't read it anyhow. But it may have helped another delusion prompted by frequent references in print to the "Satevepost." Its faintly Slavic name suggested to me that it must be a Russian newspaper, a companion, say, to *Pravda*. It wasn't until some years passed that I finally understood it to be a shorthand reference to the vastly popular magazine, *The Saturday Evening Post*.

There were other words that had incantatory effects on Walter and me, like "obelia fruticosa," which should have been the name of a lovely, exotic girl but was actually that of a kind of seaweed. And "Jejeebhoy," which suggests almost anything bizarre: a strange device, a nasty disease, or a juvenile delinquent, but which is the name of a distinguished Parsee educator—to give the rest of his name and title, Sir Jamsetjee—who played a small part in the career of Rudyard Kipling.

Walter and I were also greatly amused by certain names that seemed strange or incongruous. He had a teacher, a young woman named Nancy Blaha. That was funny enough we thought, but when she returned in the fall, a proud new bride, and was known as Nancy Blaha Murphy, we held our sides. It was, in hindsight, a combination of misguided "Americanism," fostered by new immigrants anxious to be assimilated, eager to give up ethnic names for bland WASPish ones—"Valentine" for "Vasicek"; "Livingston" for "Lipschutz"—or snobbery and youthful intolerance.

English is said to be a rather tricky language with its "to," "two," and "too," its weird "ough" construction and a host of other oddities that madden foreigners, but one must pity above all those who have to master German from the outside.

In one of his greatest bursts of humor, an absolutely marvelous, little-known essay found in *A Tramp Abroad*, Mark Twain wrote "The Awful German Language," and I shall shamelessly crib from it now to make the point. I am tempted in fact to quote it all, or even ask the editor to do himself and *Weekend* readers a big favor by printing the Twain essay instead of this, but will restrain myself!

To begin with, it's obvious that he had a love-hate relationship with German. He seems to have tried very hard to master it but never made the kind of progress he hoped for. At the start of the essay he notes dryly that at Heidelburg Castle, when he tried to surprise and please the curator by speaking entirely in German, the man "said my German was very rare, possibly a 'unique'; and wanted to add it to his museum."

The cases and genders, unknown in English, infuriated him and the complicated declensions seemed beyond human understanding. But what annoyed Twain above all was the matter of assigning genders to nouns:

In German, a young lady has no sex, while a turnip has. Think what overwrought reverence that shows for the turnip, and what callous disrespect for the girl.

Then, to make the point clearly, he translates a conversation from "one of the best of the German Sunday school books":

Gretchen: Wilhelm, where is the turnip?
Wilhelm: She has gone to the kitchen.

51

Gretchen: Where is the accomplished and beautiful English maiden?
Wilhelm: It has gone to the opera.

From there he goes on to complain about the length of so many German words often made even worse by the practice of building compounds from a dozen shorter ones. In a typical Twain mode of wild comic fantasy, he gives us this entry from his notebooks:

> July 1. In the hospital, yesterday, a word of thirteen syllables was successfully removed from a patient, a North-German from near Hamburg; but as most unfortunately the surgeons had opened him in the wrong place under the impression that he contained a panorama, he died. The sad event has cast a gloom over the whole community.

He goes on to note that "some German words are so long that they have a perspective." And he exhibits some examples, including this monster: *Generalstaatsverordnetenversammlungen*.

Then Twain suggests that "these things are not words, they are alphabetical processions." And he adds that the "dismal German system of piling jumbled compounds together" has no parallel even in our own state papers, full of gobbledygook as they are. He pounds that verdict home with this transliteration from a Mannheim journal:

> In the day beforeyesterday shortlyafter eleveno'clock Night, the in this townstandingtavern called "The Wagoner" was downburnt. When the fire to the downburninghouseresting Stork's Nest reached, flew the parent Storks away. But when the bytheraging, firesurrounded Nest itself caught Fire, straightway plunged the quickreturning Mother-Stork into the Flames and died, her Wings over her young ones outspread.

Twain correctly concedes, humanitarian that he was, that "even the cumbersome German construction is not able to take the pathos out of that picture, indeed it somehow seems to strengthen it."

He reports, with some sympathy, about an American student who, after much frustration with the language, took some comfort in having mastered, at least, the useful phrase, *"Zwei glas"* for two glasses of beer in which he forgot his despair. And the student "added with feeling, 'But I've got that solid.' "

Another American rejoiced in the word *"Damit,"* although only the sound helped since the word meant merely, "herewith."

Twain, a master-swearer, was unhappy with the German word for hell, *"Hölle."* "It sounds more like 'holly' than anything else," he laments. It is "chipper, frivolous and unimpressive." If a man were told in German to go there "could he really rise to the dignity of feeling insulted?"

This great essay is Twain at the peak of his form, which means that nothing ever printed, even by such modern titans as Thurber, Benchley, and Perelman, is better or even as good. While a slight acquaintance with German helps it's not really needed to relish Twain's humor; in fact, he supplies all the facts about the language himself, and not just painlessly, but in a way to give delight.

Finally, on the question of compound words, a joke from long ago about the vagaries of English seems appropriate. It concerns two Cockneys engaged in a dialogue about vocabulary. One complains that he ran across a word that baffled him, "category," and his companion a bit smugly explains it's just a matter of analysis—nowadays it might be called creative deconstruction.

"Look," he said. "You just break it down into words you do understand. First, 'cat'; you know what that is, of course: furry, meows, hunts mice, right? Then there's 'e,' just like in 'e an' she. And, at the end, 'gory'—that we both know; use it often enough. So the whole word is simple; it means 'A bloody 'e cat.' "

In a more serious vein, few would deny that some words have great, if often subtle, power. They can be approximated, but never equaled, by great music. Tchaikovsky does wonderfully well in his

"Romeo and Juliet Fantasy-Overture," but when Shakespeare depicts Romeo grieving over Juliet, seemingly dead, and has him say wonderingly:

> Thou art not conquer'd; beauty's ensign yet
> Is crimson in thy lips and in thy cheeks;
> And death's pale flag is not advanced there,

he does even better for the theatre of the reader's mind.
And what picture can generate the haunting imagery of Keats:

> Charmed magic casements, opening on the foam
> Of perilous seas, in faery lands forlorn.

It is beyond music or pictures.

The Sheik and I

In 1921, the Jazz Age, with its flat-chested, short-skirted, leggy "flappers" going through the rather inelegant gyrations of "The Charleston," the flashy roadsters like the Stutz Bearcat, such irreverent catchphrases as "It's the cat's pyjamas!" and "So's your old man!" and, of course, the most vital, innovative music of the century, was in full flower, much to the disgust of some diehards, both men and women, who would have interpreted the floral metaphor by muttering about a flock of blooming idiots, mainly feminine, with cropped hair and rolled-down silk stockings. Such girls, the critics complained, were bent on destroying the moral fabric of the country.

But the ferment was not slowed by such diatribes; it was even affecting quite conventional women like my mother, a fairly recent immigrant from the primitive hinterlands of Russia-Poland. So much so, in fact, that she had "bobbed"—shortened—her hair, bemusing and confusing my father, who had mixed feelings about the movement, intended mainly to "liberate" women. He approved of almost any advance away from the more oppressive Old Country abuses of wives, sisters, and daughters; but, on the other hand, not so fast! Besides, he loved her long, auburn tresses, and bemoaned their untimely passing. But he was never the patriarchal tyrant, so common then, and loving her deeply, made the best of her unnerving transformation.

As for me, I was nearly seven years old, and already an indiscriminately voracious reader, thanks to my mother, who, when I was only five, set my feet on the high road to literacy by reading to me from a book that began, emetically enough, as I see it now, "One day, when Funny Bunny Rabbit ..." Funny Bunny Rabbit! Would any story for children dare to start that way today? More likely, "One night, when Bad Ass Badger left the family burrow for his usual bit of vandalizing ..."

Like many precocious readers, I understood, if vaguely, many more words than I could pronounce, never having heard them. One of my mistakes, probably not uncommon, was to think of "misled" as "mizzled," implying a kind of induced confusion.

Well, on one evening, when my father was out of town, often the case, since he was the roving right-of-way negotiator for the Illinois Bell Telephone Company, my mother was entertaining a small group of female relatives. They sat at the dining room table, drinking tea and chatting; I was stretched out on a sofa a few feet away, reading. Actually, I was greedily skimming a book that seemed wild and wonderful, if only comprehensible in parts. It was a newly published bestseller, a real blockbuster that had, in 1921, already sold 1,194,000 copies. It was, in short, a phenomenon, discussed all over the world and roundly condemned by the clergy. It was *The Sheik* by one Edith M. Hull, a very secretive lady, it seems, about who little is known even today—not that many are interested, since she wrote nothing else of significance. The novel, written in fast moving, breathless prose, was a forerunner of today's romantic, "bodice-ripper" paperbacks so immensely popular. It was also the best of the desert-passion genre, that had got into stride with Robert Hichens' *The Garden of Allah*. It was, in a way, also an offshoot of Elinor Glyn's *Three Weeks*, of 1907, a very successful tale of illicit love.

The story told by Ms. Hull, however, in more permissive times, was definitely a bit risqué, not to say pornographic. It concerns the fate of Diana Mayo, a beautiful, cold, imperious Englishwoman, whose looks and personality bewitch (from a distance; they have not actually met when the story opens) an Arab sheik, who promptly engineers her kidnapping. That accomplished, he soon—not to put too fine a point upon it—rapes her. The language is not explicit, but the meaning is always clear, and women all over the world talked about the novel in hushed tones. But they apparently loved it, even though it obviously fed the ancient male fantasy about rape—that most women really "wanted" it.

That delusion was helped by Ms. Hull's "hero," who looked nothing like the shambling, unkempt, stubble-whiskered Yasser Arafat, implying, rather, a darker Peter O'Toole as "Lawrence of Arabia," or, at least, Omar Sharif. Further, he was immaculate, well spoken, and thoroughly deodorized. And so, inevitably, the frosty Diana falls in love, and the sheik's lawless passion is transformed into that of a tender lover. Her attraction is sharpened by a second kidnapping of the hapless girl, this time by a different sort of sheik, squat, ugly, brutal, and not terribly fragrant. He abducts her both to score against the fellow-Arab he hates, and because he too lusts for the lovely blonde.

Well, that was the novel I, as a seven-year-old, was devouring, when one of the guests, intrigued, perhaps, by the sight of a young child so deeply absorbed in a book, asked me what I was reading. Irked by the interruption, and unsure of the pronunciation, I replied tersely, "The Shee-ik." (It might be noted that only a few Orientalists knew that the word should rhyme with "make.") There were little screams and exclamations, and somebody else said to my mother, "Really, Clara—should he be reading *that?*"

"Oh," my mother said laughingly. "He won't understand it."

She was half right. Almost all the sexual innuendoes sailed well over my innocent head, and I was fascinated mainly by the exotic settings and the action, especially the actual kidnapping from one racing camel to another, of Diana, as well as her exciting rescue, much later in the story, from the "bad" sheik. The most famous sentence, one that stirred millions of feminine hearts, occurs when the sheik, shortly after the kidnapping, dumps his captive onto a huge, luxurious divan, and asks ironically as she cowers, "Must I be valet as well as lover?" I didn't get it! Not many seven-year-olds would, even today.

Oddly, experts on the Middle East said that Hull must have been there, since she had the customs and scenery down to perfection; and when one critic, John Milne, teased a woman he knew for wasting her time on such trash about an impossible hero, she retorted—the quote is from *Golden Multitudes*, about best-selling books, by Frank Luther Mott—"That's just it! The impossible man. A woman can always meet—maybe even get—the possible man. But the impossible man is possible only in the impossible story!" A literary magazine didn't agree, calling the novel "poisonously salacious."

Even those who have never read *The Sheik* probably have seen, or know about, the silent movie starring Rudolph Valentino, which was tremendously popular—again, mainly among women; men tended to be annoyed by the smarmy attributes of the lead. There were, predictably, sequels and parodies, one titled *The Shriek of Araby*, some in the movies, others in print. And, as it happens, the title of Hull's novel led to a word-symbol of the Jazz Age. Young lovers inevitably were called sheiks and shebas, made visible in the famous cartoons of John Held, Jr. These were full of mini-skirted, angular young women and Joe-college type boys with shining, slicked-down hair.

Few of them, I suspect, were a match for the novel's sheik, so tall, strong, and vital, his spotless, colorful robes faintly scented by the best Latakia tobacco, and, most importantly, as one devotee of the book put it, such a masterful love-maker, quite a euphemism for the fellow's outrageous behavior, which even aside from the kidnapping, a most serious crime, would get him about five years to life in the slammer. What 1922 American boy in his blazer and bell-bottomed trousers could hope to present that splendid an image to his flapper? He couldn't even ride a racing camel! Yet, one infers, Hull's super-Arab was probably quite at home behind the wheel of a Stutz Bearcat, or, for that matter, a Silver Ghost Rolls. And—need it be said?—he was very, very solvent.

There is a poignant epilogue to this rather lighthearted account. My mother died, tragically young, of congestive heart failure—maybe; the diagnosis was far from certain—when I was nine, and my father, who adored her and never remarried, kept her clothes and other personal possessions in a huge steamer trunk. And once, as a teenager, I opened it and explored the contents: frocks, a beaded purse, an ivory-backed hairbrush, a silver-framed mirror with a chased handle of the same lovely metal, and, near the bottom, her copy of *The Sheik*.

I picked it up, remembering, after almost a decade, a small boy immersed in a scandalous novel while my mother's guests sipped coffee and gossiped. The faint, subtle fragrance of her perfume drifted to my nose from the trunk; it was not the modern potent stuff, but more like lavender, I think. I smiled, but then, suddenly, for no apparent reason, found my eyes getting moist. I put the book back, and closed the lid. It was my last sight of the contents, because a few months later my father disposed of them and the trunk.

Despite its remarkable sales record—very high for our population then—I've not seen a copy of the book for at least forty years, and I'm not sure it ever came out in paperback. Yet, a few of its rivals, for various reasons, some clearly a matter of quality and staying power, still turn up quite often. Among them are Sinclair Lewis' *Main Street*, and H. G. Wells' *The Outline of History*. Maybe with so many romantic novels of the Barbara Cartland genre still selling nicely, a reprint of *The Sheik* might be in order. And, yes, I'd gladly accept a modest royalty for making the suggestion!

Fiction: Furry, Feathered and Finny

As a big-city boy, born and reared in some rather shabby, crowded, lower-middle class neighborhoods of Chicago, I saw few wild animals, and they were not very, living in quasi-symbiotic ways with humans. These were the inevitable grey squirrels, cute and saucy, but corrupted into cadging food; and birds, although of these I recognized only the English sparrows, small, drab, dusty and quarrelsome (not very discriminating feeders, what with their fondness for undigested grain picked from horse droppings, a large supply of which was maintained by weary brutes hauling ice carts and milk wagons); and robins, more attractive, but still so domesticated as to seem like plump, bourgeois fellow-citizens rather than free denizens of the air.

Many migratory birds must have passed through, especially in those days, more than fifty years ago, when Illinois had much more undeveloped land, but if so, they were invisible to me.

The first crack in my wall of indifference came about in a high school zoology class taught by a young, attractive woman, whose lovely voice, melodic and warm, enchanted me, so lilting it was by contrast with the strident, nasal monotones I heard from relatives and friends. When she spoke of "the common house mouse," her winsome face alight with enthusiasm, my fourteen-year-old heart was captured without a fight. She made that messy little pest seem like one of those super rodents from an Andersen fairy tale.

Ah, Miss Tyler—Gem by name, and by nature—if alive today, you are a very old lady, indeed; but to me you are still the lovely novice teacher, barely out of her teens, who first aroused my latent flair for nature, particularly wild animals in their own special habitats.

It was you who prompted me, a born slugabed, to arise for the only time in my life at four-thirty a.m. and take the long streetcar ride to Lincoln Park, there to watch for migratory birds, said to appear in large numbers at sunrise. I hoped for, and expected, orioles, tanagers, flickers, a host of wrens, and—naif that I was— maybe even an ivory-billed woodpecker, thought to be extinct.

Alas, a hopeless chump in field ornithology, I saw nothing of note and ended up photographing, with a Brownie camera, just one specimen. But I stood much too far away and the snapshot, not helped much by the cheap, distorting lens, showed a nondescript blotch that, for all I know, was another of those ubiquitous, no-account robins I could as easily have found at home—without losing any sleep.

Be that as it may, from this inauspicious beginning I became a sort of nature junkie, but mainly in a bookish way. I was no Thoreau or Beebe, spending hours and days in the field observing animals and plants. Instead I became hooked on stories and eventually had a sizeable collection. Later, I even wrote and sold two of my own to *Boys' Life* magazine. If Theodore Roosevelt had still been alive then and had happened to read them—not bloody likely!—I might have been at risk, because early in the century that choleric fellow, a giant stomping a terrified, bewildered ant, had castigated an obscure nature writer named Long, coining, in fact, the term "nature faker," to indict him. Since I was guilty of the same crime, to which I added a touch of plagiarism, T.R. would have had me cold. I had never seen in the flesh any of the critters whose adventures I chronicled with smug assurance; I merely had read about them in the works of better-qualified—maybe—authors. These included the now-forgotten ones like St. Mars and Samuel Scoville, Jr., but also the respected writers like Ernest Seton Thompson—who later called himself Thompson Seton, who knows why?—Charles G. D. Roberts, Henry Williamson and Felix Salten, who gave us the famous *Bambi, a Life in the Woods*, later cutseyed up by Disney, and sentimentalized even beyond Salten's creation, which had a few sharp edges in the novel.

Most of these were guilty of some anthropomorphism, but Seton had excellent credentials as a naturalist and was also one of the great illustrators of the genre, along with Charles Livingston Bull, who seems to have worked for every writer in the field.

Only one of these authors, Williamson, produced the real thing—literature. His *Tarka the Otter* won the Hawthornden Prize in England, awarded to writers under forty-one. It is a splendid work, far above even Salten, one of the more poetic authors. As to the others I've noted, they wrote professionally competent stories and that is all. Of course, I learned much about animals, some of it true, like the fact that although a pine marten can run down a squirrel in the tree-tops, a fisher can do the same to the marten.

All of the writers, I fear, made the animals a bit too human and some went beyond that. St. Mars, more annoyingly, had a pawky, exclamatory style full of parenthetical comments and cornball humor.

On the upper end, this small sample from Williamson, who aside from *Tarka the Otter*, *Salar the Salmon*, and other superb novels, wrote many distinguished short stories—and the mordant, brilliant, antiwar novel, *The Patriot's Progress*:

Below Canal Bridge, on the right bank, grew twelve great trees, with roots awash. Thirteen had stood there—eleven oaks and two ash trees—but the oak nearest the North Star had never thriven, since first a pale green hook had pushed out of a swelled black acorn left by floods on the bank more than three centuries before. In its second year a bullock's hoof had crushed the seedling, breaking its two ruddy leaves, and the sapling grew up crooked. The cleft of its fork held the rains of two hundred years, until the frost made a wedge of ice that split the trunk; another century's weather wore it hollow, while every flood took more earth and stone from under it. And one rainy night, when salmon and peal from the sea were swimming against the brown rushing water, the tree had suddenly groaned. Every root carried the groans of the moving trunk, and the voles ran in fear from their tunnels. It rocked until dawn; and when the wind left the land it gave a loud cry, scaring the white owl from its roost, and fell into the river as the sun was rising.

This is inspired writing, carrying out Conrad's famous directive of making us see. There are hundreds of equally good passages in all of Williamson's work, and no doubt better ones I can't spot right now. If you can find his collections—difficult, I suspect—*The Old Stag*, *Sun Brothers*, *The Lone Swallows* and *Tales of Moorland and Estuary*, you'll know what I mean.

Since no cat is ever completely domesticated, but always has a streak of wildness, I'd like to mention a great, neglected cat novel, *Rroû*, published in 1932 by Frenchman Maurice Genevoix. It is powerful, bitter and sad. Unlike Gallico's *The Abandoned*, familiar to many and excellent, and Laird's *James and MacArthur*, lighter but witty and charming, *Rroû* has been unjustly forgotten.

Not all good animal stories are fictional; Seton wrote *Great Historic Animals*, which tells about various ones that did exist and played a part in past events of interest to us. And there's the remarkable French entomologist, Jean-Henri Fabre, whose magnificent work, *Souvenirs Entomologiques*, I have in the beautiful translation of Alexander Teixeira de Mattos, who captures nicely Fabre's wonderful, lucid style. His first book, on hunting wasps, with their incredible tactics, the only one Darwin lived to see, won high praise from the titan.

But my point is that these detailed accounts of how various insects go about their complex, unthinking activities read like superior fiction. One never forgets the processionary caterpillars, which by instinct follow each other's scent trails as guides, reinforcing them as they move to various food sources, and how Fabre sneakily completed the circle, trapping them into moving continuously around the rim of a large jar until exhausted, a process that took days. It was only one of his many ingenious investigations into the blind power of such genetically fixed behavior, a near-obsession of Fabre's, and one that he and Darwin argued about in delightful letters.

Which brings me to the titan himself. Darwin's book on insectivorous plants was a pioneer effort, very interesting and still valid science. But my own favorite is *The Formation of Vegetable Mould Through the Action of Worms*. In it, after noting how huge boulders tended to sink gradually into the soil, he hypothesized that the actions of earthworms, constantly digging, eating, loosening and displacing the subsoil, caused the phenomenon; and time has proved him correct, on the whole. One delightful section in the book describes how he actually devised an intelligence test for the primitive organisms. He gave them bits of leaf, a favorite food, cut into isosceles triangles, with one apex much narrower than the other two. He wanted to know if the worms had brains enough—to put it crassly—to seize the leaves by the smallest angle, so that pulling them into a burrow would be easier. Then he kept careful count of how many interments were indeed of the energy saving kind, and analyzed the statistics. Sure enough, the smallest apex was picked a majority of the times and the difference was significant: Q.E.D.

The range of "characters" in these animal stories is truly all encompassing. My own collection, just to skim the surface, deals with the adventures (usually misadventures, for dramatic effect) of mice, shrews, moles, mountain sheep, porcupines, weasels, wild boars, trout, salmon, falcons, herons, ravens and dragonflies. Roberts wrote a whole book about a fox, and another, *The House in the Water*, about a beaver colony. Seton did one, *Bannertail*, on a grey squirrel, and also the powerful *Monarch, The Big Bear of Tallac*, the life story of a grizzly.

Not even plants are excluded. Williamson has a brilliant, haunting story about a common weed, and how it struggles for years to bear seeds while under constant attack by hoe and poison from the old-age pensioner on whose doorstep it grows—or tries to. The tale ends, ironically, with some words about "the neglected grave of Uncle Joe, upon which were growing, as though in faithful and compassionate memory, a score of little weeds of *Rumex sanguineus*." Uncle Joe was the old weed-hater—it did seed despite him—and the plants on his grave were of the same species, bloody-veined dock.

In some tales, a domestic animal—cat, dog, horse—gets involved with wildlife doings; that makes for interesting events, as when a fierce, proud, blooded stallion is cast ashore in Africa and uses its hoofs to fight off various predators. Obviously, it's much easier to empathize with such a protagonist and, in fact, with all mammals and birds, than with insects, fishes and reptiles.

But some short stories, those about higher animals, are almost unbearable in their poignancy. I'm thinking of one in particular by the gifted, eccentric R. B. Cunninghame Graham. It is "Calvary," and tells the grim story of an ordinary work horse and its terrible life and fate as man's victim. George Bernard Shaw described it as "a tale with an edge that will cut the soft, cruel hearts and strike fire from the hard, kind ones," a typically Shavian sentence, with its odd juxtapositions of the adjectives. In any case, I've not re-read it for decades, having found it too emotionally overwhelming.

As with many other kinds of writing that seem no longer of interest to TV-conditioned children, the animal story has declined in popularity, not so much, perhaps, with dogs and horses—ever of great fascination to young girls, a matter psychologists still debate—but those of the wild kingdom. That's too bad; they are great fun, and even teach us about how animals survive and flourish in their natural surroundings. Seton even went so far in one short story, "Silverspot," as to explain the crow vocabulary of calls, including some musical notation, staff and all.

To end with a typical bibliophile's observation, some of the books are very rare in first editions, like Seton's *The Trail of the Sandhill Stag* (1899), a slender volume, profusely illustrated by the author, including decorative initial chapter letters and many margin drawings. I'm very happy to own it, and have never seen another copy.

A True Love That
Seldom Fades Away

Most adults, I believe, have a sneaking fondness, partly nostalgic, for certain books they loved as children. In many cases—the Frank Merriwell saga, almost endless, going on later with younger brothers and sons, written by various authors; Elsie Dinsmore, early soap opera for kids, full of bathos and weeping; Tom Swift, with all those marvelous and impossible inventions—the prose ranges from passable to dreadful, but no matter how bad the novels were, we still remember some plots and characters, while those in better, more classic, works elude our recollections.

And there were lovely villains. Usually, they were like the proverbial winter's day—short, dark and dirty. Almost never WASP blonds, they tended to be swarthy and foreign; sooner or later the term "greasy" was attached to them. Ah, I think of Porfias del Norte, the sworn enemy of Frank Merriwell and his pals. He was a nasty fellow, but met his match in Frank, as did many other bad guys. The strange fact is that no matter how well prepared for skullduggery a murderous anarchist or Bolshevik might be, somehow Frank was ready. If the evil plotter turned out to be, as in one story, an Italian fencing master, no matter; the reader soon learns, with relief, that Merriwell had been captain of his college's team, and knew at least one tricky secret botte that enabled him to pink—he never killed anybody—the astounded expert.

Yes, there was a lot of bad writing; no wonder, considering the vast output of some popular authors. But there are a few books for children that are not only entertaining and memorable, but composed of excellent prose, indeed. I think of Hugh Walpole's three novels about Jeremy; the wonderful animal stories of Ernest Thompson Seton; and the splendid tales about Bevis by Richard Jefferies, a distinguished British naturalist. And some writers were both good and amazingly prolific, like George Alfred Henty, who specialized in historical novels for the young. They were invariably about a boy—brave, intelligent and ethical, but above all, patriotic—who participated actively in some stirring period, usually involving combat, of history. Typical Henty titles are: *The Young Carthaginian, Beric the Briton, Under Drake's Flag, With Lee in Virginia,* and *In the Reign of Terror.* How I relished them.

One of my earliest favorites was Joseph Alexander Altsheler (1862-1919), who wrote six series, each of several volumes, for boys. Some dealt with the Civil War, and his last, completed just before his death, even got to World War One. The only ones I read in their entirety, and more than a dozen times, probably, were the eight books in a sequence that began with *The Young Trailers.* This series involved five pro-British colonists, two of whom were boys, the other three being men.

The leader, because of natural endowments, was one of the boys, Henry Ware. He was tall, strong, wise in the ways of the forest, but like all such heroes, suitably modest, with no bluster. The other youth was Paul Cotter, scholarly, a little introverted, with an active imagination, not as good in the woods as the other, but brave and dedicated. In between were the older men, all carefully drawn and individualized. There was Solomon (Shif'less Sol) Hyde, a great teller of tall tales, ostensibly lazy, but always getting done what was necessary. He was second only to Ware in woodscraft. And there was Long Jim Hart, also brave and skilled, and a wonderful long-distance runner. Finally, completing the group, was Silent Tom Ross, who said little, and pretended outrage at Hyde's loquaciousness, but was quick and efficient in action. All five carried the long, deadly Kentucky rifles, and were expert shots with them. Ware was even master of the bow, and in one novel, when under disguise in an Indian village, used his skill to frustrate a suspicious brave who proposed a test to see if the stranger in the camp was actually a trained warrior.

The three men had no formal education, but were intelligent and knowledgeable. Henry had been to school, but Paul was really well read in history and literature. On one occasion, when the five were snowed in for much of the winter on an island in a lake, to which hostile Indians feared to go, since part of it was a burial ground, taboo, Cotter contrived a board with pieces and taught Sol and the others chess. They learned quickly, and soon were able to give the boy tough matches. It was also the imaginative Paul who hit on the idea of hiding, suitably cloaked, among the bodies, placed in trees, so that when the braves finally dared to inspect the island, groans from a mummy sent them fleeing in terror, never to return. They had been prodded into the attempt by the villain, present in all the books, Braxton Wyatt. He had been reared in the same little town as Ware and Cotter, and hated them, a feeling based partly on envy for Henry's leadership qualities and Paul's quiet merit. Very likely he discerned in them the four qualities he lacked, and which were esteemed by ancient philosophers: courage, fortitude, compassion and wisdom.

The intrepid quintet had many exciting adventures as they fought, almost always as irregulars on their own, against the French, their fierce Indian allies, and, on occasion, the Spaniards, out to get Louisiana away from its mostly French colonists—if they could.

And always there were the wily, courageous redskins who preferred French promises to those—equally false—of the British. Altsheler, like his five heroes, was very sympathetic in his treatment of them. He respected, even admired, their free lives, their rapport with nature and living things, and understood, while deploring, their more cruel customs. He often has Wyatt, not very good in the forest, plotting with them to confound the five rangers. Some of the Indians liked Braxton, but many despised him as a traitor and turncoat. One of the latter was the great Wyandotte chief, Timmendiquas, or White Lightning. His respect and approval went to his enemies, the Ware contingent. On several occasions he even saved their lives by going against his more bloodthirsty companions. They, in turn, wished he could be on their side instead of helping the French, for he was a noble redman, literally, being tall, strong, agile, wise, and contemptuous of wanton brutality. He was generous and large-minded, a true statesman, and appears repeatedly in the saga. In the end, when Braxton Wyatt is about to kill Henry Ware from ambush, it is Timmendiquas who fires first, bringing the series to its somber close. Altsheler, it is clear, did not wish any of the five to be guilty, even justifiably, of killing a fellow American.

Throughout the novels there is a delightful interplay of conversation: Shif'less Sol, twinkle-eyed, drawling out another odd story; Paul Cotter bringing up enlightening tidbits from history—when he tells about Alexander and his conquests, Hart remarks quietly at the end about how pointless it all was, with the young Greek dead while barely out of his teens, and questions the adjective, "Great"—Silent Tom listening speechlessly, but with deep interest. And always the author exhibits a love and appreciation of natural beauty, animals, plants, and even the seasons.

I have now only one volume of the set—*The Free Rangers*—a 1936 reprint of the 1909 edition, which I just re-read after at least fifty years, and I can say that Altsheler deserves every favorable comment I made. The story stands up wonderfully well. It is crammed with action, intrigue, good conversation among old friends, and characters, some evil, that truly come alive. The book is written in clear, grammatical, vigorous English. I can't imagine even a boy of today who wouldn't read it with pleasure, assuming he read anything more than the comics.

One of the great—and rare—pleasures of any book lover must be the chance to say, "I told you so!" For years I insisted to incredulous literary snobs, some of them English teachers, that Altsheler was not just another Burt L. Standish or Horatio Alger, but a gifted writer who happened to turn out juveniles. So I was delighted, when decades later, in a standard work, *A Critical History of Children's Literature*, by Cornelia Meigs—herself an excellent writer for the young—and others, a long, highly favorable evaluation of my old favorite met my eye.

Much as I loved the novels of Altsheler and Henty, they were, after all, boys' books, having little that could appeal to one's softer, more romantic needs, and I was becoming aware of—gulp!—girls.

All that changed when I discovered Mary Johnston. She was the daughter of a noted Confederate general, but even more the blood and bone of Old Virginia, and most of her novels derived from its colonial history.

Her first book, *Prisoners of Hope*, published in 1898, died a sudden, quiet death, but it delighted me. It opens with the arrival in Virginia of a sloop bearing convicts sent from England to be indentured servants, more like slaves, virtually. One of these is a man of good family, a Cromwellian, transported more for rebellion and political activity than crimes. He falls in love with Patricia Verney, daughter of a noble, landed, wealthy aristocrat. At first she despises him, but when he later saves her life, and has a chance to explain his past, she comes to respect, and eventually, love him. But for various reasons, any consummation is impossible, and the end is grim. Like Henry Rider Haggard, Ms. Johnston is more than a romantic writer; there are dark, disturbing little eddies in most of her novels.

But although the doomed relationship is interesting, much of the story's power comes from a wealth of supporting characters, such as a madwoman, searching for The Road to Paradise; an admirable Indian chief, who befriends Godfrey Landless—significant name—the hero who saved his life by sucking the venom from a snake bite; and the relentless, hate-filled villain, typically nineteenth century, a mulatto, believed then by many to combine the worst qualities of two races.

My own favorite was a ranting religious fanatic, a member of a tiny, extreme sect that followed one Lodowicke Muggleton (1609-1698). When Landless first sees him, he notes a branded cheek and torn ear lobes, punishments in those harsh times for being too different. He asks why his fellow convict helped an Indian:

> "The Indian needed help. Why should I not have given it him?" said Landless.
> "Because it is written, 'Cursed are the heathen who inhabit the land.' "
> "What if it had been a negro?"
> "Cursed are the negros! 'Ye Ethiopians also, ye shall be slain by the sword.' "
> "A Quaker?"
> "Cursed are the Quakers! 'Silly doves that have no heart.' "

It seems that Muggletonians hate and despise every other Christian sect; they also curse everybody not of their faith, always in the most vivid and inflammatory words taken from the Bible.

There are many exciting incidents in the novel: a slave revolt, in which Landless joins those in the Big House to protect Patricia and the others from murder, rape and pillage; Indian attacks; and the kidnapping of Patricia by the evil mulatto.

73

One of the dramatic high points occurs during the preparations to defend the house against a slave and Indian assault. Margery, the madwoman, sees in bright moonlight something she has so long sought. She saw:

> ... the white shining road cutting through the darkness and stretching endlessly away.
>
> She threw up her arms with a cry of rapture. "The Road to Paradise! The Road to Paradise!"
>
> An arrow whistled through the window and struck into her bosom—into her heart—the staff dropped from her hand, and she swayed forward and fell at her mistress' feet.
>
> The night, so placid, still and beautiful, was rent and in an instant made hideous by a sound so long, loud, and dreadful, that it might have been the shriek of a legion of exultant fiends ...
>
> "The war-whoop," said Woodson. "Close the windows, quick."

At the end, although Landless saves Patricia from the kidnapper, the political and social situation is such that her family, even with the governor's help, cannot prevent his being hanged if he returns to town, so his only hope is to be left in the wilderness where he rescued the girl. Winter is coming on, and there is almost no chance of his making it to another colony. Patricia comes to say farewell:

> "I never thought to see you again," he said at length.
>
> "I made Regulus bring me," she answered. "The others do not know—they think me asleep." She spoke in a low, even, monotonous voice, and the hand which she laid upon his forehead was like marble. "My heart is dead, I think," she said. "I wish my body were so too."
>
> "Goodbye, my life, my love, my heart," he said. "We were happy for an hour. Goodbye!"
>
> "I will be brave," she answered. "I will live my life out ... If it—if death—should come soon, wait for me—beyond—in perfect trust, dear, for I will come to you ..."

He is left alone, and hears the black rowers singing as the canoes carry away all he loves; the music fades out … and I, a boy of about twelve, wept …

As I mentioned, this novel passed almost unnoticed, but the next was another story. It was *To Have and to Hold*, and starting in 1899, it quickly sold half a million copies. Why not? It had everything expected of a romantic adventure novel: action, swordplay, pirates, flights, escapes, comradery, a great villain, and eternal love. The title plays on the words of the marriage ceremony, and the hero doesn't find it easy to hold the woman he loves.

It also takes place in the colony of Virginia, and again a ship arrives bearing, this time, young women of the service class, brought voluntarily to America as wives for the colonists, who are very short of marriageable women. Among the brides-to-be is Lady Jocelyn Leigh, who has taken the place of her former maidservant in order to escape the unwelcome attentions of one Lord Carnal—a bit obvious, for Mary Johnston!—a favorite of the king, the canting, hypocritical James I. (Yes, he did commission a marvelous transliteration of the Bible, but also broke most of the Ten Commandments—except for coveting anybody's wife, since he preferred pretty boys.)

The hero is Captain Ralph Percy, ex-soldier, combat veteran, and now owner of a small tobacco farm. He is no longer young, beginning to feel lonely, and has even thought briefly of bidding for one of the women, but a growing cynicism makes him reject the whim. When one of the wife-seekers tries to kiss Jocelyn by force, Percy intervenes and knocks him down. Then, impulsively, he offers himself as husband and protector. Desperate and afraid, the young woman accepts, but at the farm reveals herself and begs his forbearance. Although greatly attracted to her, Percy, a bit sullenly, feeling he's been conned, respects her plea, saying: "I am a gentleman, madam. You need have no fear of me."

Lord Carnal, unused to being balked, desiring both the girl and her wealth, easily prevails on the king to order her return to England, so she and Percy have to run away, braving a hostile wilderness. But not alone: here the supporting characters, as always with Ms. Johnston, play vital roles. There is Diccon, the captain's rascally but loyal servant, and the minister, Jeremy Sparrow, a reformed rogue and adventurer, a huge, powerful man who has renounced violence for the pulpit. And again, an Indian chief, a friend of Percy's. He has tamed a large cougar as a wedding gift for Jocelyn, unaware it's not a true marriage, and the big cat has a significant part in the plot.

A subtle undercurrent develops because Diccon, too, is in love with Jocelyn, and when Percy, for the first time, beats him for risking her life by disobeying his master's direct order, Diccon comes at him with a dagger. Disarmed, he is ordered from Percy's presence forever, but defiantly joins the runaways, anyhow.

As for villains, aside from Carnal, the most malignant is one of his hirelings, a small, dark, Italian physician.

At one of the novel's climaxes, the four fugitives land on an island where survival is clearly impossible. But Percy, scouting alone, comes upon a group of pirates about to bury their dead captain and decide on his successor. Having no other way off the barren, waterless island, Percy makes a bold and risky move.

Noting from the loud arguments that three men are vying for leadership, he appraises the situation and each probable opponent. There is Red Gil, a loudmouthed, bullying fellow who wields, and claims to be expert with, a saber. Then there is a Spaniard, well trained in using a regular rapier. Finally, and most dangerous, a rather quiet, even melancholy man called Captain Paradise.

Percy thinks of the woman and two friends waiting for him out of sight, and advances on the pirates: "Give you good day, gentlemen," he cries. "Is it your captain that you bury or one of your crew, or is it only pesos and pieces of eight?"

After a brief exchange, and some sharp questions, Percy tells them the treasure ship he came in has sunk with all hands: "I am a captain with neither ship nor crew. I take you, my friends, for a ship and crew without a captain. The inference is obvious."

Almost amused by his audacity, they are further amazed when he pretends to be the notorious pirate, Kirby; and following more heated interchanges, they agree that if he fights each of the three claimants in turn, and wins, he can be Kirby or anybody else, and lead them. Obviously, they don't think he can do it, and they know from his appearance he's not the famous freebooter. "I first!" roars Red Gil. "God's wounds! there will be no second!" But although the saber flails the air, and looks formidable, Percy, an expert swordsman, knows that skill is better than force in such a contest, and after a few passes, runs the brute through.

He dies while Percy is engaging the Spaniard, who claims to be the best blade in Lima; however, as Percy avers: "... but Lima is a small place, and its blades can be numbered. The sword that for three years had been counted the best in all the Low Countries is its better." Percy wounds the Spaniard slightly, then disarms him. "Am I Kirby?" he demands, with the point of his sword at his breast. "Kirby, of course, señor," answers his defeated opponent with a sour smile, his eyes upon the gleaming blade.

The third fight, against Paradise, is the most difficult, and Percy is tired; but still thinking about Jocelyn, and her fate should he lose, he outdoes himself, exhausting the pirate and finally sending his weapon flying. "Kirby or devil," the loser replies to the same question. "Have it your own way."

The pirates, perhaps because they see no point in having their three best men—only two left, now—cut each other up more, and impressed by Percy's nerve and swordplay, keep their bargain; and though further surprised by his companions, make no objections to their boarding the ship, too. So Percy sails away in charge of an outlaw crew.

There are several other exciting incidents, plenty of peril and hairbreadth escapes, but eventually Percy is cleared of all charges, and is able to take Jocelyn home, now, at last, to be truly his wife.

As for Lord Carnal, he gets almost more than he deserves, for the hapless man indeed loved Jocelyn in his own way, even to the point later of preferring her person to her wealth. Very angry on hearing about the couple's escapes from his agents, he foolishly kicks the panther, and its veneer of tameness vanishes immediately. Springing on the drunken nobleman, it tears away much of his handsome face, and Carnal realizes that without his good looks, he would no longer be of interest to King James, who would care nothing for his fate. Not that he has any choice about trying his luck again in England. Having often insulted and abused the Italian quack, a tool that failed him against Percy, the doctor finally rebels, and secretly administers a slow, subtle, deadly poison to his master; so that when the lovers do return in triumph, Lord Carnal is dying, disfigured and in despair.

And so, unlike her first novel, this one ends happily, and instead of crying, I longed to be a fighting captain who wins the enduring love of a beautiful, proud, brave young woman. I'm still waiting!

Patricia Verney and Jocelyn Leigh are typical heroines of nineteenth-century romantic novels, of which there were multitudes, but few as skillfully constructed as Ms. Johnston's. The women are passive, existing mainly as objects of love and devotion—and to be rescued. But in other romances she went further; her heroines became more independent, with lives and personalities of their own, as with the eponymous *Audrey*, a story with exceptionally somber textures beneath the basic plot.

A final comment on Mary Johnston's prose: it is remarkably good. The sentences have a nice rhythm; the descriptions are apt and evocative of Old Virginia, its people, customs and superb natural scenery; her dialogues lively, and not as stilted as that of her contemporaries. She was an expert, oddly, in depicting action, which few male authors did as well. To be sure, there is occasionally too much sentimentality, but that was the tenor of the age; few escaped it—Melville, Hawthorne, Crane—many men did not: Twain was often guilty; so was Cooper; as were scads of lesser writers. And later in her life, Ms. Johnston reformed even that tendency by turning out a few rather avant-garde novels, such as *Sweet Rocket*. But even they, like her, are mostly ignored today, and that's too bad.

One achievement that deserves to be remembered is her fine two-volume novel on the Civil War, *The Long Roll*, and *Cease Firing*, dedicated to her father, whom she apparently revered. Its set pieces about the great battles and leaders of the tragic conflict are excellent, and the sentimentality kept at a minimum.

Hooked by the Major

In 1942, a newly commissioned second lieutenant from the Officer Candidate School at Fort Sill, Okla., I was sent to Camp White, Ore., an installation still being constructed where the famous 91st Division—motto: "Powder River, let 'er buck!"—was being reactivated.

To me, fresh from Chicago, the area was a revelation. There were towering hills, splendid forests, cold, clear, fast running rivers, like the Rogue, great, heady air and marvelous icy water. There were, in season, even pears on Rogers' Ranch, said to be owned by Ginger's family, which we picked from the trees while on maneuvers. They were usually green and hard as granite, but we munched them happily. Many of us had never had access to a fruit tree, and didn't know any better until our digestive systems vigorously protested.

It was there, at Camp White, near the enchanting little town of Medford, where I found a superb barbecue lunchroom offering a food also new to me—delicious enough to startle my dormant taste buds—that I got my first assignment as an officer. Green as the whole Salinas Valley in a wet spring, I hadn't known what to expect, but vaguely assumed I'd be training recruits, giving them close-order drill, taking on marches or lecturing to them about our fine 105mm howitzers, recently supplied after years of weapons-neglect between wars.

Somewhat apprehensively, I reported as ordered to a major of artillery, part of the division brass. He turned out to be a subspecies of *Homo sapiens* familiar to me only from books and movies, a quintessential WASP. In Chicago, I had grown up almost entirely in ethnic neighborhoods, peopled by Italians, Poles, Germans, Czechs, Lithuanians, Russians and a few non-Protestants, mostly Irish. So the sight of Maj. Winton, a West Point graduate, dazzled me. He seemed the proverbial Greek god, tall, athletic, blond, blue-eyed— the blue of polar ice, I thought, as he fixed me with his gaze—and dressed in a uniform so perfectly tailored I could feel my own sagging and wrinkling on the spot.

Standing stiffly at attention, I waited for orders.

"Lieutenant," he said gravely, "we need some meat-hooks."

I must have gaped at him, for his lips twitched briefly.

"M-meat-hooks?"

"That's right. The mess officer tells me there aren't any and we have a lot of meat coming in tomorrow, so I want you to get some today."

Being "newly hatch'd" as Polonius might have put it, I didn't know I was expected to say, "Yes, sir!" and nothing else. Instead I asked, "Where do I go to get them, sir?"

The blue eyes turned chilly again and the deep, rich voice, just like that of Fredric March, said: "You have your assignment, Lieutenant; better get at it." Then, being basically a gentleman and aware of my total inexperience, he added, "I'd suggest the new construction site at the other end of camp. There should be a lot of loose metal around."

I reflected unhappily, in silence of course, that the area in question was over a mile away and, as if reading my thoughts, the major said, "There are a couple of bikes around, maybe at the mess hall. Take one of those; it'll save time."

That was enough, I knew; further questions would I be unwise, so I saluted and left.

The bicycle was a well-worn boneshaker, but better than walking. Although I hadn't ridden one for at least ten years, I managed well enough after some early wobbling; as all know, it's the kind of skill one never really loses completely.

As I sped (rather anxiously since I had no confidence in my ability to complete the assignment and could almost feel the major's glacial blue eyes drilling into the back of my head) toward the construction site, I became aware of the typical, perhaps unique, smell a training camp then—and maybe now, too—has, arising mainly, I suspect, from the sunheated asphalt of the many parade grounds and carpool lots. Even today, more than forty years later, I recall that pungent odor while visual aspects of the journey have vanished from my memory. Oliver Wendell Holmes—the autocrat, not the justice—was surely right in pointing out that the olfactory bulb, so closely tied to the brain, leaves traces tenaciously in the mind after the other senses forget the past.

When I reached the end of the map—the major was right—I found carpenters, electricians, plumbers and even a lone blacksmith complete with a fire and forge, all hard at work. I also found, and promptly "liberated," some slender iron rods used for reinforcing concrete. I felt a little guilty carrying them off, but there were many big stacks and besides, after all, everything in the camp was government property (as I was, myself, so to speak) so as much mine and the major's as anybody else's.

It was an encouraging start. But rods were not hooks, so I had much more to do, obviously, and no idea of my next move.

With all that trained help around, I should have sought advice and even assistance right there, but as a possible thief I was not sure of their reaction, so rode back to the headquarters area. There, to my relief (unjustified), I spotted a building being equipped as a sort of repair shop for the division. Inside, busily distributing equipment, was an elderly technical sergeant. I asked him if there was any kind of grinding machine around and he showed me a hand-cranked carborundum wheel. I immediately set to work—time was a-wasting, the morning almost gone—sharpening one end of a rod, a sort of trial run. I did get a rough point on it, but, alas, I completely ruined the new grinder, not built for such work. Horrified at what the sergeant might say, despite my rank, I fled and, full of despair, not knowing what else to do, returned to the construction site.

In a state of near panic, I looked for a friendly face and was attracted by the blacksmith's cheery fire. And, in fact, Tyche, the Goddess of Chance, must have been smiling, because I was very lucky. After I had blurted out my story, the burly artisan surprised me by saying that if I'd been the usual arrogant SOB officer, he'd have turned me down cold, but since I was polite and cordial, he would help.

With casual expertise, he heated several of the rods, clipped them with huge shears, bent the glowing metal into perfect hooks, and then—wonder of wonders!—even hammered the ends into remarkably keen points. The forging of Siegfried's blade could not have been more amazing to one delighted second lieutenant.

Thanking him profusely, I remounted the rickety bike and raced back to the major's quarters. When I proudly showed him a dozen splendid hooks, I expected some praise, a hearty "Good work, Lieutenant!" and maybe even a slap on the back. But fixing me with those chilly eyes, the major said quietly, "Well done, Lieutenant," and dismissed me.

It wasn't until considerably more Army experience that I understood how a "well done" was rather high praise, indeed, perhaps the equivalent in the military of a civilian boss' hearty approval.

Getting meat-hooks, admittedly, was hardly a Medal of Honor feat, and I was vastly relieved not to have returned empty-handed to meet with a scathing reprimand or contemptuous dismissal from the perfectionist West Pointer. Still, for a bookish fellow more at home with math problems than the practical, knotty ones presented by the Army, I hadn't done too badly, and the self-assurance I needed for my new rank got a helpful boost.

From then on, no matter what I was ordered to do, I never thought it an impossibility but rather a challenge to be met and, with a bit of luck, overcome.

From Bad Math Student to OK Math Teacher

For the first eighteen years of my life I was probably the worst math student who ever lived. In geometry I never understood a single proof, and I spent much class time with a compass and ruler trying to trisect angles and construct regular polygons shown to be impossible decades earlier. In my naive way, I believed that "impossible" meant merely that nobody had been persistent and lucky enough to solve the problems; it wasn't until many years later that I finally realized that when mathematicians said, "it can't be done," it can't, period. It's a logical matter, not amenable to experiment.

On one occasion, it's true, I did obtain a complicated construction for a nonagon, a regular nine-sided polygon. It was only approximate, of course, and looked like the web of a demented spider. The teacher, a sardonic and cynical fellow, happened by my desk and advised me sourly that if I put even a little of the same effort into a study of the text I might master at least the first two theorems.

As to algebra, which came next in the curriculum, I should have made the record books for sheer ineptitude. On the final exam I got ten points out of a possible one hundred and, typically, didn't even deserve them. The question, which I still recall with chagrin, asked for the derivation of a very important formula, the one for solving a quadratic equation. I didn't understand a single step of the process but somehow had memorized the text, which I wrote down purely by rote, without any comprehension of the logic involved. This modest triumph bemused the instructor, since he rightly thought that problem to be the most difficult of the exam. How did that klutz of a student get it right while bungling all the others? I never did explain, and if he's alive (not likely), he's probably still wondering.

So, how did this guy end up teaching college mathematics?

Thusly: I had a cousin, a boy of my own age, who was pretty good in algebra, and he was determined to take a free course in it, which was offered at a junior college. It was in the middle of the Great Depression, with no jobs to be had, and we couldn't afford tuition, so this was an inviting opportunity. Unwilling to go it alone he badgered me into joining him and, what with his coaching and the efforts of the teacher, a really splendid mathematician forced out of retirement by the terrible economic conditions, I actually developed a slight flair and a great respect for mathematics.

Now let me skip some years to 1942 when, with a newly acquired M.S. degree from an undistinguished Midwestern college, I was suddenly drafted. Because of my technical training I was sent to the Officer Candidate School at Fort Sill, Okla., where, in a way, I redeemed myself as to that high school exam by making a perfect score on the final for potential second lieutenants. It was nothing to brag about, since the material was elementary—nothing more advanced than trigonometry—and I was, after all, a Master! In any case, I spent most of the war teaching the simple math needed by artillerymen.

Actually, I'd originally intended to become a chemist. However, I soon learned I was not only ham-handed in the laboratory but too impatient to conduct careful experiments. In fact, I might have been a most remarkable researcher, since I often managed not only to spill solutions all over the table but somehow make compounds combine to form messes hitherto unknown in the field. In any case, I shifted my major to math.

Behold me next, in 1945, teaching college math at night in a church-affiliated school in Chicago. Both in the Army and here I was able to confirm what most teachers soon learn: there is no better way to master any subject than to impart it to others. But there was many a near-traumatic experience along the way.

On one memorable occasion it was bittersweet or, rather, sweet-bitter. Confronted suddenly one evening with the trickiest calculus problem of a set—one I hadn't even assigned!—I ploughed into it, sweating, and covered the blackboard with a jungle of symbols for most of the ninety-minute session. Even after forty years I remember the gist of the problem: a light is moving away at a constant velocity from a sphere of given diameter. How fast is the illuminated area increasing at a particular time?

When by skill and luck I came up with the right answer, as given by the author, the class applauded me—how sweet that was! But during our next meeting I got the bitter part when a young female student handed me a scrap of paper on which her husband, an engineer, had solved the same problem in about three lines. Although I felt like crawling under my desk, I did try to explain that it's one thing to tackle a problem alone, with paper and pencil, free of pressure, and another to solve it handily with forty sharp eyes following my every step, each false move, and any hesitation.

After three years in Chicago, with its murderous winters, humid summers and autumn air loaded with ragweed pollen, I escaped to Southern California, where, invincibly ignorant, I had the temerity to apply for a position at a small, prestigious private college. Since its staff had been decimated by the war, and they were still short of math teachers, I was hired temporarily, although any Ph.D. would have been far more to their taste.

Since I didn't drive and housing near the campus was both scarce and expensive, I had to get up at five in the morning and ride ninety minutes to make my eight a.m. class. The streetcars were ancient, drafty and far from immaculate, but offered free courses in human types and behaviors. I still can recall clearly two specimens that intrigued me. One was an elderly man, a regular on my own ride, who had the loudest, most dreadful hacking cough I've ever heard. How he coped with it and didn't ever get well still baffles me. Then there was a middle-aged woman, somewhat overweight, yet not enough to explain her truly elephantine rear, which took up enough seating space for three ordinary people.

One advantage of this tiresome commute—another ninety minutes returning home—was that I learned to study my lecture material and even grade papers on the streetcar—an occupation that often intrigued other passengers.

As to the job, I was far out of my class, and totally misplaced. The upper class students, with their immaculate grooming, low, melodious voices and immense self-assurance, regarded me, I'm sure, with at best a kindly condescension. My mother died when I was nine and my father never remarried. With one arm and four sons he was not all that good a catch, alas, although a kind and loving father who did his best. But I had none of the social graces, having been reared in a masculine household. My clothes sense was nil, my voice a nasal monotone. Aware of that, I tried to compensate by extremely careful articulation, which must have seemed pedantic and affected. So the pupils thought of me, I was sure, as the King Arthur's nobles did the Connecticut Yankee in Mark Twain's novel: something like an elephant. It was a powerful beast, able to do things they couldn't, but as for being an equal—I should smile! as Twain would have put it.

One of my first classes was a disaster. I was solving an assigned problem in analytic geometry and made the same mistake as in the

Chicago school; I did it the hard way, taking much too long. As I finished, I heard a pert coed—poisonously, deliberately audible—say: "He did it just to show how good he is." Blushing deeply, I stammered out that I'd actually overlooked the simple solution, one using midpoints instead of the complicated distance formula, but whether anybody believed me is doubtful.

Eventually, my students came to respect me, but it was hard going at first. A second debacle then made things worse; my immediate superior, a cultured, gentlemanly, capable Ph.D., suddenly died of a brain tumor and I had to take over several very advanced classes in fields of math I'd never even studied. Luckily, by hard work and judicious selection, I managed to keep a few pages ahead of the pupils, but it was a very rough semester.

My last teaching assignment before dropping the profession to write was both more suitable to my abilities and more pleasant; it was seven years at a junior college in Los Angeles. There, my M.S. and modest attainments were at least adequate for the curriculum.

Looking back now, some reflections seem in order. To begin with, mathematics is for the young. Most great creators in the field were brilliantly productive in their teens; I was much too old at eighteen to begin learning the fundamentals. That fatal delay was compounded by attendance at inferior colleges with teachers who were not really creative mathematicians but, at best, competent instructors.

Yet, ironically, I had—and still have—a passionate love for the subject and would rather be truly good at it than write a bestseller or even another *Adventures of Huckleberry Finn*. And, contrary to popular belief, it is not dry and boring, a matter of memory and tiresome calculations, but alive with beauty, wonder, elegance and a host of intriguing mysteries. One of the greatest, it should be noted, is the amazing fact that equations relate so closely to the "real" world. How does it happen, for example, that when James Clerk

Maxwell, the superb physicist, derived the famous equations for the electromagnetic field they foretold the existence of radio waves, then unknown? Philosophers of science still debate such matters.

I can't convey the joy I felt when making a few small, even trivial, discoveries. To find and prove something never before known must be like writing a good poem or composing a fine little sonatina almost worthy of Mozart or Ravel.

It used to be thought—I'm sure my geometry teacher believed it—that the study of mathematics also taught logical, rigorous reasoning in other fields. That is demonstrably false, as shown by many irrational, not to say imbecile, comments over the years by distinguished scientists. But I will say this: that writing out a mathematical research paper, however minor, with proofs and explanations, does indeed tend to refine and clarify ones expository powers. Mathematics is, at least, the most nearly unambiguous language we have.

Finally, my writing career was tolerably successful. Between 1950 and 1965 I sold more than 260 stories, mostly in the fields of detection and science fiction, to national magazines; many were reprinted and anthologized repeatedly. I was able to use mathematics in some of the plots, a useful ploy, since my shtick was one gimmick per story.

I learned how to write, not from courses, but by playing the "sedulous ape" to Stevenson, who did the same to Addison, Kipling, Doyle and others who were masters of narration, if not characterization. It has been rewarding and fulfilling but, to be honest, I'd rather have solved the enigma of Fermat's Last Theorem, a problem that has baffled the best mathematicians for centuries.

A Not-Very-Mighty
Hunter Confesses

My career as a not-very-mighty hunter was sporadic, shameful and guilt-ridden. It began, I think, when my parents took my three brothers and me to Lincoln Park in Chicago. I was eight years old; it was my first trip there, and I was fascinated by the splendid lagoon, with its brushy shores, dimpled waters ruffled by the breeze and its many waterfowl.

With a child's desire for a secret place of his own, I burrowed deep into the undergrowth near the water, and settled down in a leafy, warm, fragrant hollow. As I lay there, feeling hidden and secure, a female duck, probably a mallard, came by, leading a brood of her young. Few birds are more endearing than ducks, and the babies are irresistible. Yet, moved by some vagrant, atavistic impulse, some stirring of hunter-gatherer genes, I picked up a large twig and flung it at the family. To my surprise—and horror—it turned out to be a deadly move; there, pitifully floating sideways, clearly dead, was a fluffy little duckling.

Terrified, I scrambled out of the brush, certain that I had committed a serious crime and that if found out would be hauled off to the nearest police station. That didn't happen, of course; nobody ever knew, and I didn't confess even to my younger brother, normally my confidant in almost every action I undertook.

Even now, over sixty years later, I despise the child I was and consider his act deplorable. Why? Why did I have to kill that little duckling? I still don't know, and never shall. Ironically, life being overfull of ironies, for many years before I became a vegetarian my favorite dish was roast duck, which I relished far more than beef, lamb or pork.

The next victim of my hunting prowess was a hapless sparrow, one of the dusty, brown pests that proliferated in the Midwest then. Like pigeons today, many of us considered them as winged rats. They throve mainly on horse-droppings, full of undigested grain and plentiful, thanks to milk wagons and ice carts, each drawn by a patient, often overworked, underfed, animal.

This was about two years after my first crime, and I was now the owner of a cheap air rifle—a BB gun, as we kids thought of it. From the back porch of our third-floor flat, where I had infuriated at least one grouchy neighbor by random plinking (a few pellets having rapped her windows), I spotted an English sparrow on a phone wire about twenty yards away. It was my first chance at a living target, and although I didn't really expect to make a hit, I had to shoot. It was my second surprise—maybe I had hidden gifts as a marksman—since the little bird fluttered briefly and fell to the ground.

Greatly excited, even exultant, I raced down the stairs and hurried to the site. What I found there reversed my mood fast. Guilt—crabgrass of the emotions, and even harder to quell—struck again. From a small hole in the sparrow's breast, blood was oozing, terribly red and real. I hated myself, and wondered again why I had fired so casually.

Next came an interlude during which nothing died at my hands, although I did my best to kill—not bird or beast this time, but a fish. I had an uncle, a man least likely in the world to seek an outdoor avocation, it might seem. He was the quintessential salesman, outgoing, totally citified and hyper as to words and motions. Nevertheless, he invited me and my kid brother to join him for a day's fishing in the Fox River, hardly more than a creek but thought to have a fair supply of perch.

He drove us to the site, helped us load a pair of cheap rods with bait—worms, I think—bought locally, and the three of us sat on the wooded bank, looking like the real thing. It soon became a bore; we not only caught nothing, but didn't get a nibble. It baffled me that my uncle seemed so happy. It wasn't until years later that I understood his need to relax, and that fishing of this kind is, above all, relaxing to the nth degree. Not the catching, but the waiting, musing, dreaming, and resting are what give fishing its appeal to most people.

Behold the great hunter next in the Army; Camp Roberts in 1944, to be exact. A brand new second lieutenant in the field artillery, I was invited one Saturday afternoon to join three fellow officers on an expedition to the desert with some .22 rifles used for training, being cheaper to fire than the Springfields and Garands. Just what we were to shoot at, I didn't know, and doubt if they did, either. But there must have been something out there, crawling, running, hopping or flying, to be targeted. And there was: vultures, graceful, soaring, hovering, sizeable, and we thought—mistakenly, as it turned out—rather easy to hit. Our efforts were probably illegal, even then, although I'm sure these were not condors, but ordinary buzzards. In any case, bloodthirsty as we were, the big birds, 600 feet or more aloft, were invulnerable, even moving in a lazy, slow way. No doubt we didn't realize how long the range was, particularly for a .22 slug.

Frustrated, my companions sought out an easier victim and soon found one—a large lizard sunning itself on a rock. The unlucky reptile was only a few yards away, a point-blank target, and the captain, taking careful aim, could hardly fail this time. The result was unedifying, to understate the case; the lizard was splattered into a bloody mess. I felt a little sick at the sight. At that moment, I think, my desire to kill anything—anything with blood, at least— began to die.

My last sorties as a hunter occurred in Laguna Beach, where I lived and wrote for two years. I now had two really good pellet-guns and began to take them to the rocky beach early in the morning for target practice. Doubtful that it was legal to fire them in the city limits, I went quite early and chose the most deserted areas where I could spot any approaching cop in time to hide the two pistols.

At first I was content to shoot at bits of flotsam in the surf, and was not above throwing in a chunk of driftwood to aim at. But I soon found living targets, the small crabs that scuttled cautiously among the huge, crevassed boulders that extended to the waterline. They were not only moving erratically, and so a challenge, unlike the drifting objects, but actually fragmented when hit, being very brittle. More often than not, they lived and escaped after losing a few legs. My conscience didn't bother me—much—since there was no blood and, after all, crabs are like big insects, almost immune to pain, I was sure. But it did begin to gnaw, subtly, vaguely at the start, then more strongly. The crabs were alive and might be enjoying that to some degree, if not quite as much as the murderous oaf firing at them. So, not to belabor the point, I just gave it up, never again to deliberately kill anything but flies, which I hate venomously, and mosquitoes, which I'd be willing to spare if only they'd shut up.

Now, rather paradoxically, I can't oppose all hunting, since I revere logic. I detest, as do all true sportsmen, the slob hunters, who shoot at anything that moves before being assured it's not a cow or a fellow human unlucky enough to be crouching or vaguely deer-like in appearance; who destroy farmers' property, leave gates open so stock can wander onto the highway and get killed by cars; and who strew their garbage all over the landscape. Some of these fools never dream of zeroing in their rifles in advance of season's opening, then take impossible, 600-yard shots at running game, wounding more animals than they kill cleanly. They are also responsible for too many fires.

But as to sane, humane hunting by people of good will and competence, I cannot fault the practice, knowing that few, if any, animals in the wild die peacefully of old age. If they are not somehow culled, normally, naturally, by predators, they perish even more miserably from starvation or disease.

I don't care to do the necessary killing myself, but *de gustibus non est disputandum*, and if some people enjoy hunting and are good at it and don't go after endangered species, who am I to play the outraged moralist? Obviously, if it were possible to let deer, bears, cougars, coyotes and wolves maintain a natural balance of animal populations, I would then oppose all hunting. But since the present situation is clearly quite artificial, an elk might as well be shot to death as starve. And, if as is often the case, some or all of it is eaten, so much the better.

There are, to be sure, plenty of controversial offshoots of the whole hunting mystique. Take the question of game preserves. Is it right or sportsmanlike to raise normally free ranging and wild beasts like cattle on fenced ranches, and then sell permits to hunt the partly tamed animals? When, and with what species, should dogs be used—as in the case of cougars—to run down or tree the game? Since it's unlikely that large, powerful, intelligent animals like elephants would not die natural deaths if unmolested by man, do we have a right to kill them? The same question applies to whales, but the hunting of them seems about to end for good soon.

I don't claim to have all the answers, but feel emotionally, perhaps instinctively, that we should give the benefit of the doubt to most of the beautiful, noble, harmless, innocent animals with which we share—uneasily, at times—this overstressed planet.

John Barleycorn, Nick O'Teen and Me

In his little-known, but powerful and moving 1913 testament, *John Barleycorn*, Jack London told the grim story of his long battle with alcoholism. Although the title comes from folklore and actually refers to the personification of malt liquor—beer, ale, porter and such—in the book itself, the concentration is more on whiskey, especially of the cheap rotgut sort used by the lower classes.

Even today, nobody knows for sure what causes alcoholism, although a genetic factor seems to be involved. In London's case, his impoverished, loveless childhood may have aggravated any inherited weakness.

As for me, my skirmishes with John Barleycorn were few and non-traumatic; in fact, I never really liked the taste of alcohol, preferring by far what seemed to me then, and even now, the king of beverages, a thick, creamy chocolate malted, available in my youth for fifteen cents and consisting of at least two big glasses poured from a metal flask after much agitation by an electric mixer at the soda fountain.

I was influenced by my father, who had a naive faith in prohibition until gang wars, rum-running and corruption raised doubts even in his mind. All his life he expressed dislike and fear of alcohol, except for a little wine at family gatherings where it would have been churlish to abstain. Oddly, this didn't prevent him from raising his splendid, if untrained, baritone voice in such saloon favorites as "How Dry I Am," "Show Me the Way to Go Home" and a mournful ditty about a new bridegroom who had to refuse attending a bachelor party with the plaintive observation, "I would if I could, but I can't." ("Why?" ask his pals.) "Because I'm married now."

My first significant encounter with John Barleycorn came when a new friend, Martin Schwartz, invited me to have lunch at his house. I gladly assented and, having lost my mother several years earlier when I was nine, had no great gourmet expectations, so that the baloney sandwiches on rather dry bread didn't impair my healthy appetite.

However, when I looked about for the big glass of milk that usually accompanied lunch sandwiches at home, there was instead a bottle of beer. Horrified, I asked Martin if there were any other choice, like chocolate phosphate or even a nice, lime-flavored soft drink named Green River.

Martin was amazed. His family came from Europe, where the notion of preferring milk to beer was like asking a Frenchman to give up champagne for ginger ale. He urged me to at least try a sip. Gingerly, I did so, and almost spat it out, so unpleasant it seemed to me. Looking back now almost sixty years, I have to smile, since literally the only alcoholic drink I now enjoy—rarely, alas—is beer. Not the thin, lite, chemical-filled junk so common in this country, but the dark, heavy, rich potent brew imported from England as ale, and from Germany as just good beer.

My next grapple with Mr. Barleycorn came in the Army, where as a new officer at Camp Roberts, I found a vogue for the mixture called rum-and-Coca-Cola, inspired, no doubt, by a popular song sung by the Andrews Sisters. Since I couldn't refuse to join in when glasses of the stuff went around of an evening, I had to drink a little, finding, rather to my surprise, that it was quite good, thanks to the Coca-Cola, which masked the alcohol taste I still disliked. In any case, I never had more than a few sips, so didn't comprehend what it felt like to get tipsy, much less falling-down drunk, which happened all too often to some of my fellow officers—especially old-timers of the so-called "regular Army," who for some reason were very heavy drinkers. The veteran non-coms were even worse, seemingly unable to function without large amounts of beer and whiskey.

After the war, I had no reason to drink and didn't, except, as always, for a little wine at social affairs or dinners out. But there was a brief interlude that left me with mixed feelings about alcohol. While visiting my aunt and uncle in Los Angeles, I was offered some apricot brandy and politely tried it. I was hopeful, because a ripe apricot has always been a favorite fruit. Alas, I could detect little of that flavor in the liquor; as usual, the alcohol overpowered whatever the fruit may have contributed.

My third—and last—encounter with J. Barleycorn was also my first and only loss. I went down for the count. It happened thusly:

At that time I had been selling regularly to *The Magazine of Fantasy and Science Fiction*, edited by the polymathic opera-buff, Anthony Boucher. As it happened, his associate editor, J. Francis (Mick) McComas, came to Los Angeles and invited me to have lunch with him at a posh hotel in Beverly Hills. Of course I was delighted to accept and, still years short of owning a car, went by bus.

Mick turned out to be a burly, genial, cynical Irishman and, as I soon learned, a drinking man. The moment we were seated by the waiter, he ordered a martini, asking me what I'd have. Knowing less about mixed drinks than a pig does about Plato, all I could do was ask for the same, which apparently confirmed him in believing I was a kindred spirit, a guy who knew the right stuff to go in a glass.

As I sipped—thoughtlessly, unaware of the liquid TNT I was downing—he was already ordering another "… and the same for my friend!" It never occurred to me—how could it?—that my stomach was still very, very empty and the martini very, very dry and generously poured, since the fancy hotel was charging a pretty price per ounce.

In short order, Mick chugalugged no fewer than five of the potent mixes and I, still the wide-eyed innocent, flattered by his jovial attention, followed suit. It was after number four that I found my eyes crossing, my speech slurring and my hand-motions wavering. In fact, although I didn't realize it until some hours later, I was, for the first and only time in my life, drunk. Mick, I might add, was not; he had the traditional copper-lined stomach, perhaps.

The rest of the afternoon, including the expensive food, is, to this day, a blur; but somehow I got through it, lurched to a bus and got back home. Shortly thereafter, my eyes uncrossed, I was again steady on my feet and I had learned something—that getting drunk is not really much fun.

Nowadays when I indulge, which is about twice a year at most, my taste is thoroughly corrupt, at least, by the McComas standard, that of all who take drinking seriously. I enjoy only such dreadful stuff—as they would see it—as Alexanders, in which it's really the chocolate I relish and not the alcohol—and maybe a daiquiri (which I'm not even familiar enough with to spell for certain!) for the fruit flavor, if that's what it is. And, of course, my beer-a-year. Martin Schwartz, if you're still alive, I owe you an apology.

Oddly, when it came to tobacco, which unlike liquor, has almost no redeeming qualities, my father had no bias. It's true he looked down on cigarettes and had no interest in pipes; but greatly enjoyed fat, mild cigars of which he smoked exactly three daily, one after each meal. I realize now, something few knew then, that it was a relatively safe choice, especially since he didn't really inhale. But

Nick O'Teen, called a god by Kipling, is ever and always a dangerous and subtle master.

My three brothers and I rather enjoyed the fragrant odor of Dad's cigars and two of them later became smokers, but not so wisely, opting for cigarettes and pipes. In my case, I was lucky from the start, having even less truck with tobacco than with alcohol. Many of my friends began smoking early, while still in their teens, but I was tempted only once, trying a popular brand of cigarette called Melachrino. All I got was an unpleasant, stale-ash taste and never had another.

Today, my most vivid memory about smoking is that of my father, who occasionally told us, with much amusement, an experience he had while doing phone company business in a tiny Illinois town named Zion. It was ruled, iron-hand style, by a religious eccentric who was not only a sincere, dedicated geoplanarian—the town had an official, stated belief in a flat Earth—but had convinced the inhabitants to shun liquor, tobacco, jazz and dancing. His name, I recall, was Wilbur Glenn Voliva.

On this occasion, my father was quietly enjoying his after-lunch cigar when he was stalked by a shrill-voiced harridan, who then swooped down to snatch the offending Ben Bey from his lips. As he gaped at her, the woman, whose kiss, to use one of his pet quotes, would paralyze a shark, screamed, "You stinkpot!"

Like all of us who are not George Bernard Shaws or Oscar Wildes, he suffered from *esprit d'escalier*, that depressing afterthought about how we should have responded with a brilliant witticism, instead of the feeble cliché we actually did mumble. My father, he ruefully admitted, had no such biting retort, but merely told the woman to hurry home and look after her unfortunate husband instead of harassing a harmless smoker. Those were, after all, the days of male dominance, when a wife was supposed to be housebound, meek and probably pregnant. So Dad missed his chance to come up with a real zinger like, "Why don't you find a dark corner somewhere, woman, and just quietly ovulate?" Or, anticipating a famous putdown of the acidulous Lady Astor by Winston Churchill: "Look, Ma'am, I can stop smoking any old time, but tomorrow you'll still be rude, ugly and stupid!"

She was a bit of an aberration then, a woman feisty enough to take on not merely a smoker, but a dominant, lordly male—and in public at that; but today, I suspect, her name is legion. Which is fine with me: turn-about is fair play.

A Different Fear of Water

A great American poet—there are very few such after the magnificent Emily Dickinson, alas—who preferred to live in England, Thomas Stearns Eliot, the centenary of whose birth is upon us, promised to show us "fear in a handful of dust." Well, why not? That shouldn't surprise anybody; medical dictionaries have enormously long lists of phobias, many so bizarre as to amaze mere laymen. They range from acarophobia, fear of worms—not, as one might infer, a problem for fishermen, since it relates more to a parasitic infestation of the skin and the resulting itch—through nosophobia, fear of illness, which most of us have at times, to zoophobia, fear of animals, which means the patient may have to vacation at the Poles, keeping a wary watch for white bears, or the most sterile parts of the Gobi Desert. So I've no doubt that in some list, suitably Latinized, is dustophobia, fear of dust, not altogether unknown to some housewives!

The more common fears are often discussed even in popular magazines: fear of confined spaces, of height, of the dark, of leaving home, or even a particular tiny room, of water—not just the sort that led recently to the death by drowning of a hapless Navy recruit, forced to submerge by overzealous instructors, but the terrible reaction of rabies victims to the sight or sound of water—and, of course, sheer terror at the presence of snakes, spiders, and other creatures thought to be creepy-crawly. Even photos cause panic.

Having had some excellent basic courses in zoology, I was never afraid of snakes, finding them dry, not slimy, gorgeously colored, graceful as all get-out, and rarely aggressive, preferring to flee from humans if given half a chance. Oh, there are a few exceptions, like the South American bushmaster, a sort of Don Rickles of reptiles, forever in a fury; and the Indian cobra, perhaps unhappy over the dreadful climate and worship of scrawny cows instead of—what else?—hooded snakes. And I approved of spiders, since they killed flies, which I did detest. But any student of nature comes to realize that among living things beauty is truly only skin deep: anything that functions perfectly and with elegance must be considered beautiful in its way. That means toads, slugs, and even parasites like tapeworms. I admit, however, that as a child, I was wary of hornets and bees, but any sensible person walks wide of irritable yellowjackets. And I shared with other kids of my generation in Chicago the terrifying delusion that dragonflies, which we called "ear-sewers," would, if provoked, actually sew one's ears closed. Their long, slender, flexible abdomens did indeed suggest needles ready to get surgical, so we tended to flee when one of the insects flew near us. But once having outgrown that superstition, I found them to be lovely, with flashing, sun-refracting wings ablaze with rainbow colors. And what superb fliers! They can go forward, backward, and even hover like hummingbirds or tiny helicopters, a rare ability among winged creatures. And they are relentless fly-killers, snatching them in mid-flight with astonishing dexterity. I liked that, since there were far too many of the pests about, especially in summer. These days, I note with regret, dragonflies, like so many birds and other insects, are comparatively rare, perhaps because ponds have been paved over, and flies greatly reduced in numbers.

Lest I be accused of inconsistency, having denied much ugliness among living things, I admit that a big bluebottle, shining in the sun as if clad in burnished armor, is rather pretty, but I loathe its buzzing persistence and lack of personal hygiene. There is nothing so noxious that a fly won't happily alight upon and tramp over it. And as to wiping even one of its six feet on leaving the mess, forget it! It's a pity flies don't have an underwater stage so that the grim dragonfly nymphs, so powerful and ravenous that they even kill and eat small minnows and tadpoles, can't get at them.

One uneasiness, well short of a real phobia, but distressing at times, that I shared with a few other perceptive kids, might be called fear of the void. It had two related aspects. By day, lying on our backs, we would look up at the sky and suddenly feel as though nothing held us to the Earth, and that we might somehow "fall" upwards, which seemed, oddly, "down" from that position, into the vast, endless blue expanse.

The feeling was much stronger at night, however, when all the stars were out. Then the nagging fear that gravity was an illusion that might fail us, allowing a terrible plunge up/down into that dreadful emptiness, so cold and Stygian, got so intense we would jump to our feet, and talking much too quickly, get back to more mundane, trivial matters.

Finally, I come to the real point of all this—fear in a puddle of water. This was much closer to a phobia, at least to a small child, whose eyes were nearer the water. The apprehension began when an older boy, a bully, scared some of the younger kids by asserting that even a tiny pool on the street was really bottomless, no matter how shallow we foolishly assumed it to be. Of course, if a child bent over, and jabbed a finger through the reflecting surface, they would quickly dispel the illusion, but little children are not logicians. More convincing, by far, was the fact that if one peered down, the water seemed to have no bottom, but opened unhindered to endless depths, a chasm of menacing blue. Even some of us who were older had some doubts at first, and for the very young, seeing is believing, literally.

On one occasion, still vivid in my memory, the bully held a writhing, wailing eight-year-old over a large puddle, and smirking evilly, threatened to drop him "through," "down," "up," or whatever direction was appropriate, for a long, terrible fall to the unbounded space shown in the water. It ended, of course, as such incidents usually do: the bully, suddenly aware that his victim's screams were bound to bring adults to the scene, put the child down, reproached him for taking a little joke so seriously, and sidled off.

Now, since anything that happens to a future writer, especially during his most impressionable years, those of childhood, is almost certain to turn up sooner or later in some work, it's not remarkable that *Alfred Hitchcock's Mystery Magazine*, almost fifty years after the event, published one of my best horror stories, "Puddle." And by one of those highly improbable coincidences that so puzzled Carl Gustav Jung, who constructed a complex theory about what he termed "synchronicity," while I was writing this essay, I received word that the story will be reprinted for the first time.

Except for a few childhood friends, I've never met anybody who suffered from puddlephobia, but I suspect there are some around. And although I quickly lost that irrational fear, I'll confess that even today, when the sky is bright and clear, and I find a puddle in my path, even a mere film of water that reflects the menacing, infinite blue above, I may hesitate for just a microsecond before stepping into it …

The View From Rudyard Kipling's Toad

In one of his earliest verses, an immensely talented author named Rudyard Kipling neatly pinpointed a pervasive moral flaw found in almost every society. The significant quatrain occurs as a heading to the satirical poem, "Pagett, M.P.," about a fatuous, pompous, insensitive member of Parliament, who was also a "fluent liar." Here are the lines:

> The toad beneath the harrow knows
> Exactly where each tooth-point goes.
> The butterfly upon the road
> Preaches contentment to that toad.

The cocksure Pagett, abrim with complacent ignorance, refers to India's dreadful heat as the "Asian Solar Myth" and is full of many other misconceptions about a subaltern's life in the teeming colony.

Most of us who have lived a half-century or so can readily look back on countless occasions when we have played the role of that know-it-all butterfly, and have participated in what could be called thoughtless cruelty to toads. Not only have I been guilty myself, but have observed a great many more instances of such conduct by others, and even when aware of the injustices and wanton sneers, lacked the guts to speak up about them, much less vigorously denounce them.

I am far from being alone in this sort of social poltroonery. It's obvious that most such unconscious offenses relate to race, gender, age, class and appearance, including that of a handicapped person.

Let me, in a spirit of impartiality, indict myself first. When I left my job as a mathematics instructor at Los Angeles City College in 1957, I was given a modest send-off by my colleagues, and, as usual in such circumstances, was expected to make a short speech, which I did. Unfortunately, moved by some vagrant whim I still don't understand, and can't explain (it was an odd shift from my normal behavior) I began with a bad imitation of a catchphrase then very popular on TV made so by one Bill Dana, who played the role of a naive Hispanic. Facing my expectant fellow teachers, I said, "My name ... José Jiménez." There were a few chuckles, and some blank looks; my colleagues probably watched more PBS shows than network variety programs.

But the failure, in part, of my comedy attempt is not the point. Not until days later did I suddenly realize what that kind of humor did to a Hispanic faculty member, a highly intelligent, amiable, generous and kindly man. He was the toad beneath the harrow, and what then seemed to me like a harmless, casual joke was lacerating to a degree an outsider couldn't comprehend. How I learned this is irrelevant, but it's a fact, and the only positive result of my gaffe was that from then on my antennae were more sensitive to such slights.

One hears these days quite often from bewildered whites the query, why black groups, organizations? We don't have a White Caucus, so why a black one? These plaintive questions show again that not being under the harrow bars true empathy. Tigers don't need to unite against goats, so how elitist and exclusive and unnecessary it must be for goats to organize. After centuries, first of actual bondage, and then extreme discrimination, blacks have every reason to feel a "unite or perish" impulse which the dominant class obviously doesn't understand. Clearly, I submit, a matter of white— cabbage?—butterflies preaching contentment to blacks under the harrow.

Another personal experience, which clings in my memory like a burr, took place in the shabby Los Angeles apartment house where I lived at the time. The manager, a young woman, was an alcoholic, which may explain in part why she solicited bribes from prospective tenants; apartments were scarce then, right after the war. She was also a snoop and petty thief, who entered the rooms when the occupants were away, examining personal possessions and stealing some to sell for booze money. But it should be added she was neither malicious nor deliberately callous, but had impulses of admirable generosity.

On this occasion, I was chatting with her one morning, when a recent friend of hers, a new tenant, approached rather unobtrusively, so that the manager didn't notice her, and happened to make a grossly anti-Semitic remark. The woman was Jewish, and I saw her face, normally calm and serene—she was a pleasant, rather shy person—seem to crumple into a mask of pain. The manager caught some of that, and went into an agony of remorse. "Oh, I didn't mean—" she began, but the tenant, almost running, reached the entrance, and left the building.

There was a somewhat similar situation when I was at Camp Roberts. As adjutant of a battalion, I knew a little more about the personnel than most, and witnessed one moment of poignant irony. A captain, a battery commander, was praising, very enthusiastically, his executive, a lieutenant. The man was competent, bright, dedicated and generous with time and money. The battery was lucky to have him. He then discussed another officer, calling him a tight-fisted, devious, lazy, conniving sort, ending with the smug comment that all Jews were like that. In fact, as I knew, the fellow he despised, although he "looked" Jewish, was actually from Lebanon, and the blond, husky lieutenant he so admired was indeed a Jew. Did I say anything? No, but not in this case from lack of moral courage; rather I realized at once that if I told the captain the truth, he would, like all bigots, immediately reverse his judgments, and find the executive a nasty type after all.

Outrageous insensitivity, or just another instance of thoughtless cruelty? That is the question I still ask myself about the commandant of the military academy where I briefly taught math and science. Ironically, he was a decent, well-meaning, straight arrow guy, yet I saw him commit an unforgivable act of inhumanity. I was in his office, along with a young man who had been hired a few weeks after me. He had what could only be called a deformity, if a minor one: a monstrous boat-hook of a nose, much bigger than the one familiar to viewers of *M*A*S*H*. It was also a good deal ruddier than his face, and had visible pores. It seemed he had tried to cash a personal check in town, a small southern Illinois community, but the cautious manager wanted identification, and had called the commandant to confirm the instructor's identity. On being asked what the new man looked like, the commandant quipped, no doubt thinking it was funny, "Oh, he has a tiny nose." I could hear the bank manager exclaim, "What?" sure that he had been conned by a check forger. Then the commandant explained, and the two agreed on the teacher's appearance. As for him, I could see the shame and misery on his face, but since he must have needed the job, he said nothing.

I was deeply embarrassed to have witnessed this, and still can recall the scene in vivid detail. As for the commandant, he was unaware of what he had done, and went on with business as usual, dealing in turn with each of us.

Had the toad actually complained, the butterfly, amazed, would have assured him airily that no harrow-point had really bloodied him, and that he mustn't take such harmless humor so seriously. The silent scream from the victim as the steel barb nipped him didn't reach the commandant's inner ear. I suspected he had been injured many times before, with never a butterfly to notice. I didn't get to know him well enough during my short stint there to suggest a rather obvious solution: plastic surgery, which was fairly cheap then, a good rhinoplasty being available for under $300. (But it was much less common and thought a frivolity by many.)

One very early toad-butterfly incident takes me back over fifty years to the small, not-very-distinguished college in Chicago where I was a student. Those of us majoring in math and science were, of course, in a time of male dominance in such fields. Almost all boys, a group of us gathered daily after classes in the gym, where we compared notes on the travails of chemistry, physics and math, with much waving of slide rules. No women were usually in evidence, but one day a girl wandered in and proceeded to act rather unwisely. She was not attractive—to understate the case—and had, oddly enough in view of my theme, something of a toad-face. But she was young, fresh, seemingly bright and did have an excellent figure. Looking back now, I infer she was starved for male company and had probably had few if any dates in her brief life of perhaps eighteen years. She began to act very girlishly flirtatious, vastly overdoing it, so that most of us were embarrassed and tongue-tied, not knowing—those were more innocent days for young men—how to respond. But one student, thought to be somewhat of a sophisticate compared to the rest of us, a handsome, suave, self-assured fellow with a reputation as a lady-killer, suddenly turned to the girl and said in a clear, well modulated, almost caressing voice, "Your trouble is you're boy-crazy!"

There was dead silence in the room. Her face turned bright red, and her shoulders sagged. Then she whirled and fled. The insult was uncalled for, however silly her behavior. Obviously, the butterfly was unable to empathize with the needs and desperation of a young woman socially isolated and yearning to be accepted, liked, even loved. A few of us reproached him, but the general feeling, I regret to recall, was relief that she had gone, leaving us to our male concerns. For any inclined to echo the butterfly and wonder why all the fuss, I should point out that in those days to call a girl "boy-crazy" was much worse than terms used now like "tramp" or "bimbo."

I believe the general situation has improved much since then. For example, people who address paraplegics in wheelchairs no longer seem to assume that they are mentally retarded, and must be talked down to. And more of us are ready to admit that some people are on the streets not because of indolence or fecklessness, but rather owing to a drastic shortage of affordable housing, complicated by the fact that often where apartments go begging—in Dallas, say—there are no jobs.

There is also more understanding of why a young, unmarried girl from a dysfunctional family, desperate for some love and caring, may foolishly become pregnant. In short, our society as a whole reacts less like Pagett, M.P., and tends to empathize with the toad under the dangerous harrow.

A particularly terrible harrow still vivid in our collective memory is the Vietnam War. Nobody, not even an aging survivor of Guadalcanal and Iwo Jima, two jungles of World War Two where the fighting was desperate and very bloody, can fully comprehend what it felt like to be under the unique iron teeth of the Viet Cong. Nor can any of the books, movies or TV specials, even when supervised by combat veterans, lift the veil completely. Kipling, I believe, had it exactly right: only the hapless toad, hugging the

112

ground as the great, insensate rake bears down on it, knows—truly knows, with every neuron in its body—where each metal prong is heading and the terror it evokes, when there is no escape, and that a humble, beneficent little life is at risk.

Perhaps the most smug, insensitive butterflies I know of personally must have been the arrogant young interns at a famous teaching hospital in Chicago during the early 1930s. Like so many doctors, they were far better with technique than insight and compassion. Sent out, as part of their training, to deliver babies among the poor, largely black, people who lived near the hospital, they found it highly amusing when some young woman, full of gratitude for their help, exulting over a fine infant, would shyly offer to name it after the intern and he would instead, suggest a new, offbeat name, sonorous for a boy, mellifluous for a girl. They all came direct from a medical dictionary and included such gems as Rigor Mortis Jackson, Melanoma Wilson, and Acne Rosacea Harris. The mothers, many quite illiterate, were delighted. No further comment is needed, anti-nausea medicine, ad lib.

Even today, obviously, we are far from living in Arcadia, although such behavior would be regarded with revulsion. And having begun with Kipling, we might well end with another great, if totally different kind of author, Alexander Pope, whose quatrain supplements that of his British successor:

But times corrupt, and nature, ill-inclined,
Produced the point that left a sting behind,
Till friend with friend, and families at strife,
Triumphant malice raged through private life.

"Triumphant malice"—there is a lot of it around, but I'd like to think that Pope's acerbic view is somewhat outdated, that we have more feeling for creatures under the harrow, but I'm by no means sure, as we enter the twenty-first century, that it can be completely refuted. And I seem to hear a querulous objection, a modern perversion of Mr. Dooley's Irish wit of a century ago: "Don't be in such a hurry to hand out justice to them toads—we ain't got enough to go around among us butterflies!"

In Praise of
Sir Henry Rider Haggard

Sir Henry Rider Haggard—what a rhythmic drum-roll of a name!—
is remembered today, if at all, by two of his inferior novels, *She* and
King Solomon's Mines, that were made, several times each, into not-
very-good movies. I say "inferior" not because they aren't fun to
read but because his other romances are distinctly better. All his
novels, in fact, maintain a wonderful atmosphere of fantasy,
adventure, suspense and a kind of deeply rooted melancholy that
gives them remarkable depth at times, an insight into the tragic
human condition in which brave men die futilely and love cannot
always conquer.

Haggard, whose writing was respected by no less a long-time
correspondent of his than Rudyard Kipling—himself a great master
of English—did not have a brilliant style, but wrote a solid,
workmanlike prose, especially good with action, description of
terrain and the interactions of African peoples, particularly—timely
today—the Boers, a fierce, independent, pious, tenacious and
fanatical group.

Their long and bloody struggle with the Zulus, a people equally
proud, courageous and capable of great cruelty as well as
generosity, forms the background of Haggard's best romances,
those which feature his hero, Allan Quatermain—not

"Quartermain," as too many careless reviewers give the name. He is a small man, wiry and agile, but notable chiefly for his skill with a hunting rifle; in fact, with most firearms of the day. Yet he is much less one dimensional than that description implies; he has humor, irony, wit and moments of self-doubt that almost verge on anti-heroism.

Quatermain appears as a major character first in the fine prequel trilogy, *Marie*, *Child of Storm* and *Finished*, which deals with Boer-Zulu relations, mainly violent. There is, however, a touching love story woven into the action. Allan loves Marie, a daughter of Boers who don't actively dislike the Englishman but prefer that she marry her own kind. Complicating the relationship is Mameena, a Zulu maiden who loves Allan but is clearly beyond the pale as a possible wife, or even mistress, given the social milieu of the period.

The three novels make up a magnificent saga of adventure, star-crossed lovers and ethnic struggles as the Zulus fight to keep their land and identity while the Boers seek to escape British domination, both military and cultural.

Needless to say, both Mameena, the lovely, hapless, gallant black girl (whose name means the wailing of the wind) and Allan himself, lose out in the end. She dies trying to save Quatermain, and his beloved Marie also perishes tragically.

A dramatic high spot of the novels occurs when Allan is put in the terrible position of having to kill a giant king vulture—a very difficult shot—with his rifle, or die horribly at the hands of the brutal Zulu chief, Dingaan. Of more concern to Quatermain is that Marie, and most of the Boers, also have their lives on the line.

The Zulu chief explains: "I did not say that you were to be killed, Macumazahn,"—Allan's name in Bantu—"it depends on whether I find you to be a liar, or not a liar ..."

He goes on to discuss the claim that Quatermain is "one who can shoot birds flying on the wing with a bullet, which is impossible. Can you do so?"

"Sometimes," Allan tells him, and Dingaan makes his bet. There is a Hill of Stones where evildoers are slain, and when they are dead the vultures come to devour them. If the Englishman can kill three out of the first five on the wing, he will spare the Boers; if not, he'll kill them all, but keep Marie as a wife—something clearly intolerable to Allan.

In almost all of the novels about Quatermain, supporting characters reappear, like Hans, the little yellow Hottentot, a faithful friend and ally, if given to petty thefts and connivings. It is he who persuades Allan, despondent over missing the first shot, that the better method is to fire at the birds' tails since it is sight of the flash that startles them. The bet is won by a hair.

There are always excellent minor characters very nicely drawn, like Vrouw Prinsloo, the earthy, outspoken Boer matron who loves Marie, and wholeheartedly wants her to marry Allan, defying the group's leader, Piet Retief, a real-life figure from history who features in *Marie* and is still canonized in South Africa by the right-wing whites.

One of the most striking and unforgettable of Quatermain's allies in many of the romances is the Zulu loner, almost an outcast, Umslopogaas, who is introduced to the readers in the great "lost race" novel, *Allan Quatermain*. In it, Allan, an Englishman named Good and the grim, sardonic Zulu search for and find a previously unknown civilization in a remote part of Africa reached only after a terrifying journey on an underground stream and past a pillar of fire that almost roasts them. It is typical of Umslopogaas' imperturbability that as they skirt the searing flames he calmly munches antelope meat; after all, why die hungry?

The lost race is ruled by two queens, one dark, the other light, a familiar symbolism; both would like to have Allan as a consort. The dark monarch, abetted by evil priests, plots to depose and murder her sister, the good and gentler of the two rulers.

Before all that, however, Haggard describes Umslopogaas:

> He was a very tall, broad man, quite six foot three, I should say, but gaunt, with lean, wiry looking limbs ... he was a "Keshla," or ringed man—that is, an adult, seasoned warrior, so identified by an intricate, gummed hairdo—and he had a great, three-cornered hole in his forehead. (This last the result of an early, almost fatal, combat.)

Umslopogaas fights with a unique axe, a huge, murderous weapon of ancient, mystical origin. It has a rhinoceros-horn handle, and the Zulu wields it expertly; in his hands it is a fearsome device.

As it happens, the novel climaxes with his death at the top of a giant staircase, which he defends in a gallant, hopeless battle in order to give Allan time to save the good queen from her sister's army. However, Umslopogaas continues to appear in many later novels since Haggard, like all writers—one thinks immediately of Sherlock Holmes—is always free to report events that happened when he was still alive.

The big, dangerous Zulu is more than a killer, however. He is a thoughtful, melancholy, often witty man with insights very useful to Quatermain. Most readers can't get too much of him.

Haggard's approach to plot structure is interesting. Before developing the main theme, he not only introduces many of the important characters but involves them in a secondary, but revealing, action-event. For example, in *Allan Quatermain*, before the lost-race search is well under way, Allan, Umslopogaas and Good stop at a mission station where they are hospitably received and much taken by the little blonde daughter of the missionaries. When the child is kidnapped by the Masai, who want the three turned over to them—having had the worse of an earlier encounter—Allan plots a raid to recover her. But first Umslopogaas addresses the chieftain who has brought the ultimatum:

> ... thrusting his fierce countenance to within a few inches of the Masai's evil, feather-framed features, he said, in a low, growling voice, "Seest thou me?"
>
> "Ay, fellow, I see thee!"
>
> "And seest thou this?" and he held Inkosi-kaas (his great axe) before his eyes.
>
> "Ay, fellow, I see the toy; what of it?"
>
> "Thou Masai dog, thou boasting windbag, thou capturer of little girls, with this 'toy' will I hew thee limb from limb. Well for thee that thou art a herald, or even now would I strew thy members about the grass."
>
> The Masai shook his great spear, and laughed long and loud as he answered, "I would that thou stoodst against me man to man, and we would see," and again he turned to go, still laughing.
>
> "Thou shalt stand against me man to man, be not afraid," replied Umslopogaas, still in the same ominous voice. "Thou shalt stand face to face with Umslopogaas, of the blood of Chaka, of the people of the Amazulu, a captain in the regiment of the Nkomabakosi, as many have done before, and bow thyself to Inkosi-kaas, as many have done before. Ay, laugh on, laugh on! Tomorrow night shall the jackals laugh as they crunch thy ribs."

The raid is a splendid account of action and, indeed, Umslopogaas meets the Masai chieftain, catching him in flight.

Haggard is clearly intrigued, it should be noted, by the huge, unique axe so terribly wielded by the Zulu. Its name means "chieftainess," and in addition to the big, steel blade, always kept razor-keen, it has a sharp prong. With that, occasionally, instead of slashing, Umslopogaas would make a single, adept, lethal stroke to an opponent's head, a tactic that earns him the nickname "Woodpecker."

This is a superb adventure story from start to rousing finish.

In the Quatermain books, Allan appears not only in nineteenth-century Africa, but in other countries and even other times, usually by means of a hallucinogenic herb, taduki, which when smoked in appropriate surroundings, regresses one, mentally, to some past existence. Quatermain thus has adventures in ancient Egypt and Ice Age Europe, although he is still always the pukka Englishman, and temperamentally and as to character, remains much like his African persona. He also often has allies similar in their natures to Hans and Umslopogaas, if of vastly different races and backgrounds. In one of Haggard's last romances, Allan even meets "She," but that is back in Africa and as himself.

Two of the best novels about Quatermain are *Allan and the Holy Flower* and *The Ivory Child*. In the first, he is hired to help an English orchid collector find a giant specimen that is considered holy by a remote tribe deep in Africa. This adventure climaxes on an island, the home of an old, giant ape, which also is revered by the tribe and used as an executioner. Presumably disarmed, Quatermain and his friends should be easy prey to the mighty brute, but the villains didn't figure on the ever-wily Hans, who has concealed a rifle-barrel in a hollow walking stick and the stock in a big ball of native tobacco. The firearm is Allan's little rifle, Intombi ("The Maiden"), highly accurate but light and of too small caliber for the ape. And, unfortunately, the Hottentot, feckless as well as clever, has allowed most of the ammunition to drop out of a hole in the pocket of his tattered jacket.

Predictably, the huge primate, white-furred with age but still more than a match for ten unarmed men and used to helpless victims, attacks. But Quatermain, the gifted marksman, saves them ... although, as Wellington reputedly said after Waterloo, it was a damned close-run thing.

A gripping story of high adventure, if not so credible today now that we know about gentle gorillas.

Haggard also wrote a number of romances that don't involve Quatermain. One of these is *Cleopatra*, his individual treatment of the fabulous charmer. It is, like much of his work, dark and tragic ultimately, a story of a fatal obsession. It tells how a young novice priest forgets his vows, his country, everything because of his infatuation with the enchanting but deadly queen, a woman lovely and as life-destroying as one of those poisoned Florentine daggers.

He also wrote a purely science fiction novel, not his forte, which normally centered on fantasy. This was *When the World Shook*, hard to find in a first edition and harder to believe than any. It concerns a vengeful scientist, angry at the world, who plans to punish it by making the Earth wobble violently in its orbit, something to be accomplished by running a giant boulder through a vast tunnel beneath the surface—a notion that would make Newton blink.

The Ivory Child is superb. It takes place in an unknown part of Africa, of course, and in it, just as Allan lost Umslopogaas in the epic stairway battle, he has to watch Hans, his companion since boyhood, killed by the demonic rogue elephant, Jana, a one-tusked monster of near-supernatural powers. The elephant attempts to winkle Quatermain out of a rocky shelter; Hans diverts the beast and is tossed and trampled to death. But Allan escapes—and weeps bitterly, without shame, for the little Hottentot.

As with *Allan Quatermain*, Haggard plots expertly, beginning the novel in England, where Allan is trapped into a shooting match against a most unpleasant *arriviste* and scoundrel; this at a typical estate with its game reserve full of pheasants and doves. Although Quatermain is not familiar with these and doesn't have his own guns, he wants desperately to win, his opponent having fleeced him years before. The suspense is beautifully built up, the climax surprising and Allan's skill tested to the utmost.

Haggard was amazingly versatile and wide-ranging as an author; aside from his romances, he wrote several "serious" novels, not very good, alas, but also a number of fine yarns not involving Quatermain. There is, for example, *Eric Brighteyes*, based on familiar Norse mythology, but effectively and freshly told. It is a grim, brooding story with hints of the supernatural, much in a Twilight-of-the-Gods mood. The plot elements, the adventures of Eric, are all his own; only the Nordic background is borrowed. An incident of high drama occurs early when Brighteyes, who asks to attend the wedding of the woman he loves but cannot have, is told by her father, who hates him, that if he comes via a terribly dangerous, icy mountain path that no man had ever mastered he will be welcome. So, naturally, Eric does just that.

And there is *Red Eve*—the title refers to a valorous, independent woman, one of many whom Haggard, apparently a cryptofeminist, has in his novels—a medieval romance; and *Morning Star*, also historical, set in ancient Egypt.

Of the same genre and exceptionally readable is *Margaret* (originally published in England as *Fair Margaret*). Set during the reign of King Henry VII, this novel is the story of an English girl who is kidnapped by an amorous Spaniard who carries Margaret off, much against her will, to his home country, where it is learned— horrors!—that she's a heretic. When he will not renounce her, the church accuses her of witchcraft and hopes to burn her. Her English lover, Peter Brome, goes single-handedly to the rescue. Oddly, for so serious a novel, it has a lot of Haggard's typical dry humor. A most entertaining story.

Worth at least a mention is *Nada the Lily*, an account of Umslopogaas' first and only love. It is a somber, haunting tale, tinged with the supernatural, as exemplified by such entities as ghost-wolves and a witch-mountain. As Allan lost Marie, so the Zulu loses Nada. A weird, twilight, strangely sad story.

It's a companion piece, in a way, to *Allan's Wife*, a novella collected in *Allan's Wife and Other Tales*, a book of Quatermain stories published in 1889. Like the Sherlock Holmes tales that confuse us about Watson's wife or wives, it manages to puzzle us as to just how Marie, and another woman who had his son, Harry, relate and fit in chronologically—something I've never figured out for sure.

Other instances of Haggard's great range of eras and times are legion. They include *The Ancient Allan*, featuring Quatermain in Babylon; *Wisdom's Daughter*, a third book about Ayesha, or She-Who-Must-Be-Obeyed, to use her full title; and *The World's Desire*, in which he collaborated with Andrew Lang, a distinguished man of letters and collector of fairy tales. The last concerns the further wanderings of Ulysses with Helen of Troy in ancient Egypt. Other books are *Queen Sheba's Ring* and *Moon of Israel*, about the Exodus; *Montezuma's Daughter*, a treatment of Aztec society; *Heart of the World*, about a Mayan city under a lake; and *The Virgin of the Sun*, more South American fantasy-adventure. Finally, one of the best of his lost-race tales is *The People of the Mist*, in which there is a spectacular escape from the villainous priests (as usual!) by riding flat stones down a glacier and across an awesome gulf in the ice.

An interesting sidelight is his mystical adventure novel *The Ghost Kings*, in which he consulted no less a master than Rudyard Kipling.

Quite intriguing is the fact that Sir Henry also wrote a nonfiction work of sociology, which might still be relevant (I don't really know, never having seen it) what with the hugger-mugger in South Africa. It is *Cetewayo and His White Neighbors*, which analyzes and explicates race relations in that troubled part of the world.

Haggard wrote a lot, obviously, and most of it was out of print for many years. Not long ago some of the rarest novels were reprinted in England—lovely books, too—and may still be available. They include *The Wanderer's Necklace*, *The Brethren* and *The Yellow God*, all very hard to find until these reissues.

It's a pity, I believe, that young people today don't know these superlative novels of high adventure, crammed with action, intrigue, suspense, fantasy, humor and exotic locales as well as accurate history. And I long for the day when some wise producer will give us a really good film version, one that closely follows Haggard's careful plotting, superb balance, wealth of fascinating characters and high moral tone. The solid ethical considerations that underlie the actions of his heroes are often overlooked, but are very admirable. My choice for such a movie would be—by a hair, since there are so many candidates—*Allan Quatermain*, which has it all: African adventure with Umslopogaas, a lost-race theme and, of course, Allan Quatermain.

The Prose Style of Hector Hugh Munro

Anybody with even a casual interest in classic short stories is sure to know "Saki," Hector Hugh Munro (1870-1916), whose contributions to the domain of such fiction are unique in their combination of offbeat plots, wit, sly malice, black humor and glittering prose style.

Like the work of O. Henry, they have in many cases surprise trick endings; but, in addition, a great deal more, including Swiftian satire, insights about British caste and class, and sophisticated, allusive dialogue. Such famous little gems as "Tobermory," about a cynical talking cat; "The Open Window," a tour-de-force dealing with a young girl who lies brilliantly and to great effect; "Sredni Vashtar," a fine conte cruel; and "The Reticence of Lady Anne," with its shocking denouement, have frequently been anthologized. But the 600-odd pages of his collected stories have dozens that are as good, but less well known. Some of those are "The Quest," a hilarious spoof of Christian Science; "The Schartz-Metterklume Method," which puts down educational theorists of the over-naive kind; and a delicious assault on permissive mothers and spoiled brats, "The Storyteller."

All his writings abound in aphorisms, nothing like those of Poor Richard, but heartless quips more like the best of Oscar Wilde with extra dollops of venom. But they avoid the bitterness of Ambrose Bierce somehow, having a sort of cheerful infusion of unreality that makes them more amusing than offensive.

A few choice specimens would include the most famous:

She was a good cook as cooks go; and as cooks go, she went.

Hating anything in the way of ill-natured gossip ourselves, we are always grateful to those who do it for us and do it well.

And this, about a girl too greedy for a peach to be generous or even fair:

But Agnes was fat first and good-natured afterwards; those were her guiding principles in life.

Finally, as politicians know:

A little inaccuracy sometimes saves tons of explanation.

Munro also invents wonderful names: Ada Spelvexit, Miriam Klopstock, Arlington Stringham and Sir James Beanquest are typical.

He died much too young, killed in the senseless meat-grinder of World War One in November of 1916. Even on that incredibly horrendous battlefield, he maintained his sense of humor, albeit dark and nihilistic. On Christmas, of all days, 1915, he wrote a verse in his usual vein of anti-religious cynicism:

While shepherds watched their flocks by night
All seated on the ground
A high-explosive shell came down and mutton rained around.

His stories, however, have been analyzed by numerous critics far better qualified than I, but there is another work of his, long out of print, that is little known but very interesting. It is the novel—novella, actually, being, like his only other one, *The Unbearable Bassington*, quite short—*When William Came*. This is a predictive story written just before the war started that tells about a nonviolent takeover of England by the forces of Kaiser Wilhelm, the "William" of the title. It is a somber account, relevant today, when so many once-free nations have been invaded or dominated by bigger, more ruthless ones, yet the gloom is illuminated fitfully by Saki's irrepressible wit.

The Germans are not portrayed as monsters; they are nothing like the Soviets in Afghanistan or the holocaust-makers in Cambodia; rather, they are trying, after the quick collapse of British forces at sea (not because they are inferior in courage or training, but simply too few for a better prepared enemy and on land against overwhelming numbers and more modern equipment), to impose Prussian discipline and order on the unruly, inept, lazy, pacifist Britons. The actual fighting is of very short duration; literally, a matter of days.

As the novella begins, we meet one of the more passive accommodative people, those who hope they can pursue their own interests despite the situation, ignoring the invaders, rather than actively opposing them. She is Cicely Yeovil, whose husband—the real protagonist of the story—is due back after years abroad. He has no real notion yet as to the oppressive nature of the occupation and gets his first taste on taking a cab:

... Yeovil turned to give direction to the driver.

"Twenty-eight, Berkshire Street."

"*Berkschirestrasse, acht-und-swanzig,*" echoed the man, a bulky, spectacled individual of unmistakable Teuton type.

"Twenty-eight, Berkshire Street," repeated Yeovil, and got into the cab, leaving the driver to re-translate the direction into his own language.

For obvious reasons, artists are more likely to conform than other citizens, since they believe, reasonably enough, that their work is independent of military and political benign occupation. Nor are there many courses of action for the British. Some choose exile; others resist, but in a low-key, stubborn, cultural way, and ostracize the Germans. Most conform, hoping that time will solve the problem, which is also what the invaders expect—that eventually the English people will become much like the solid, hard working, patriotic, military-minded Prussian elite.

The bewildered Murrey Yeovil, who has been almost incommunicado in the hinterlands of Russia for many months, later gets a rundown about the brief, disastrous conflict. An old friend, Dr. Holham, explains:

"It started," said the doctor, "with a wholly unimportant disagreement about some frontier business in East Africa ... then the negotiations over the affair began to drag unduly ... the papers reported a highly menacing speech by one of the German ministers, and the situation began to look black indeed ... 'War between two such civilized and enlightened nations is an impossibility,' one of our leaders of public opinion had declared ... by the following Friday the war had indeed become an impossibility, because we could no longer carry it on ..."

And then Holham talks ruefully about the vast superiority in ships and men, the latter untrained or only half-trained in the English forces. The enemy, he adds, were a nation hardened to arms, and we, the British, not even the idle apprentice:

"There was courage enough running loose in the land, but it was like unharnessed electricity, it controlled no forces, struck no blows ..."

A bit later Yeovil asks:

"Are you trying to tell me that this is a final overthrow? ... Are we to remain a subject race like the Poles?"
"Let us hope for a better fate."

The doctor then adds that if Germany ever becomes involved in a naval war with another great power, and affairs were at a critical stage, England might be offered independence in order to keep its latent hostility under control. But he admits that won't happen in the foreseeable future.

Of the compromisers and opportunists, one of the more completely treated by Munro is Ronnie Storre, a protege and hanger-on of Cicely's, a very good looking boy, a forerunner of Evelyn Waugh's youths, who is greatly talented as a pianist. Another is Tony Luton, a music-hall performer, selfish and out for the main chance. When Cicely is asked about Storre's profession, she replies with cool irony:

"He has a great many friends who have independent incomes."

Later she adds:

"... he's just a boy who looks nice and eats asparagus."

Even more well-rounded is Herr von Kwarl, a sort of political adviser, with no official position, to the German government:

The stupidity of his mien masked an ability and shrewdness that was distinctly above the average, and the suggestion of brutality was belied by the fact that von Kwarl was as kind-hearted a man as one could meet within a day's journey.

In the novella, he observes and philosophizes about British reactions to the occupying forces, and what they might portend.

There are many poignant scenes, one of the best occurring when Storre plays his anticipated recital for a largely German audience. As he completes the first part, Canon Mousepace—another marvelous Saki name!—says:

"It is a great gift, a great gift," chanted Canon Mousepace. "You must put it to a great use. A talent is vouchsafed to us for a purpose; you must fulfill the purpose. Talent such as yours is a responsibility; you must meet that responsibility."

And Munro's comment:

The dictionary of the English language was an inexhaustible quarry, from which the canon had hewn and fashioned for himself a great reputation.

Then from one of the German royalty present:

"You must gom and blay to me at *Schlachsenberg*," said the kindly-faced Landgraf ...

Storre plays again and the room is filled with applause. A duchess says to Yeovil:

"... isn't it just glorious?" she demanded, with a heavy insistent intonation of the word.

"Is it?" said Yeovil.

"Well, isn't it?" she cried, with a rising inflection. "Isn't it just *perfectly* glorious?"

"I don't know," confessed Yeovil; "you see, glory hasn't come very much my way lately." Then before he exactly realized what he was doing, he raised his voice and quoted loudly for the benefit of half the room:

" 'Other romans shall arise,

Heedless of a soldier's name,
Sounds, not deeds, shall win the prize,
Harmony the path to fame.' "

As the audience gasps, looking at the German guests, Tony Luton has his own revelation:

"Hell!"
The word rang out in a strong young voice.
"Hell! And it's true, that's the worst of it. It's damned true!"

And not long after, we learn that the opportunist who had tried to accept occupation had abandoned his first really big break on the stage, and had signed on as a deck hand in the Canadian Maritime.

In a moving scene on a train, Yeovil has a conversation with a countryman off for some fishing, who first tells him how he dislikes Germans and then, flamboyantly, brags about how England will recover and drive out the enemy. When Yeovil points out how the navy is gone, and that the Germans outnumber the few ships in overseas ports by more than ten-to-one, the boaster says:

"Ah, but they'll build. They're only waiting to enlarge their dockyard accomodation ..."
"And do you suppose," asked Yeovil in slow, bitter contempt, "that the victorious nation is going to sit and watch and wait till the defeated foe has created a new war fleet, big enough to drive it from the seas? ... Who is going to protect Australia or New Zealand while they enlarge their dockyards and hangars and build their dreadnoughts and their airships?"

Very angry, the fisherman says:

"I've listened to you long enough ... Fact is, I'm an out-and-out patriot and you're only a half-hearted one ..."
"England has never had any lack of patriots of that type," thought Yeovil sadly; "so many patriots and so little patriotism."

How did such a catastrophe happen to Great Britain, at that time (1913) thought to be perhaps the strongest country in the world? It's impossible to tell the whole story of even a short novel in a mere essay, but one more quotation gives some hints:

"They grew soft in their political ideas," continued the unsparing critic; "for the old insular belief that all foreigners were devils and rogues they substituted another belief, equally grounded on insular lack of knowledge, that most foreigners were amiable, good fellows, who only needed to be talked to and patted on the back to become your friends and benefactors. They began to believe that a foreign minister would relinquish long-cherished schemes of national policy and hostile expansion if he came over on a holiday and was asked down to country houses and shown the tennis court and the rock-garden and the younger children ..."

Sound familiar?

At one point, when von Kwarl is asked what will keep the English quiet while they are being Germanized, he says:

"The hopelessness of the situation ... Every wave that breaks on her shore rattles the keys of her prison ... If every German was flung out of England tomorrow, in three weeks' time we should be coming in again on our own terms ... not a shipload of foodstuff could reach the country."

And when the friend says to von Kwarl that compulsory military service must be instituted—at present the British are humiliated by not being allowed to serve—and that it will infuriate them:

"Remember, they have made great sacrifices to avoid the burden of military service."

"Dear God," exclaimed Herr von Kwarl, "as you say, they have made sacrifices on that altar!"

Of all the moving, evocative little vignettes in this short novel, my own favorite takes place at the home of an exiled Englishwoman, who has fled to a Far Eastern country, presumably a colony of Great Britain's, with her five children. It is a primitive society, hot and dusty, depressingly different from the cool, green fields of the homeland she loves and misses. Her French visitor questions her. Just why did she come here? There are kindly natives, lovely tropical flowers, all the exuberant growths of such a clime, but—

"In all this garden that you see," said the Englishwoman, "there is one tree that is sacred."

"A tree?" said the Frenchman.

"A tree that we could not grow in England."

The Frenchman followed the direction of her eyes and saw a tall, bare pole at the summit of the hillock. At the same moment the sun came over the hilltops in a deep, orange glow, and a new light stole like magic over the brown landscape.

And, as if they had timed their arrival to that exact moment of sunburst, three brown-faced boys appeared under the straight, bare pole. A cord shivered and flapped, and something ran swiftly up into the air, and swung out in the breeze that blew across the hills—a blue flag with red and white crosses. The three boys bared their heads and the small girl on the verandah steps stood rigidly to attention. Far away down the hill, a young man, cantering into view round a corner of the dusty road, removed his hat in loyal salutation.

"That is why we live out here," said the Englishwoman quietly.

It seems clear that Saki overestimated the benevolence of the Germans as occupiers. To be sure, they were not Nazis and the level of their culture in 1913, as exemplified by their science, music, art and literature, may have been the highest in the world. But neither were they a nation of peaceful, tolerant Danes. The brutal invasion of Belgium, even if the atrocities were mainly Allied war propaganda, was a violation of a major treaty solemnly entered into;

and the first use of poison gas also made a sizable blot on their record. Those lay ahead and Munro didn't foresee them—who could?—but there were some obvious hints from German behavior in East Africa, where they administered their colonies with extreme ruthlessness.

The novel, it should be noted, is tainted with the low-key, upper class anti-Semitism typical of the times; though there is not really much of it compared to other writers.

And so—Hector Hugh Munro, pointlessly dead at forty-five, probably well short of his peak as a writer, too young to die, yet surely too old for frontline duty. At his age he needn't have volunteered in 1914 at the start of hostilities; there were not yet the horrendous casualties that came later, far worse than in any conflict in our day. But it was a time of hyper-patriotism, with much talk of a short war; nobody foresaw the grim future.

What a pity; what a waste!

Victor Hugo's Loose Cannon

A phrase often heard these days, usually from people concerned about the Iran-Contra affair, is "loose cannon." Some of those who employ it most glibly misunderstand what it means, and talk about wild firing, as if visualizing a belching muzzle hurling shot and shell at random about a ship's deck, killing or maiming the crew wholesale.

That notion is totally incorrect. The kind of ordinance involved was never easy to fire even intentionally, could go off by accident only in rare circumstances; and if and when it did, expelled a single iron ball, unless charged with one of the fancier loads like chain shot or langrage, the latter a mass of bolts, nails and other bits of metal. In any case, being a muzzle-loader, it could fire only once before being recharged, a slow and complicated procedure.

Actually, the whole problem of the runaway iron monster arose from a natural desire on the part of admirals to acquire the same kind of awesome firepower long achieved by field artillery and siege guns. On early ships-of-the-line this was done, rather poorly, by encasing the gun barrels in wooden troughs. When fired through holes in the ship's side, these jerry-built contraptions would recoil in a clumsy, erratic way, sliding back some feet, often ending up at an angle. They then had to be manhandled back into position for the next round.

The next advance, a rather obvious one, was the use of carriages with wheels, at first wooden, then iron. The whole assemblage, which might weigh a ton or more, had to be carefully restrained, because Newton's First Law was paramount, and one of the great guns would recoil with immense force. So it was tied down with chains or heavy ropes of manila or hemp, which kept it from rolling back more than a few feet, after which the gunners had to muscle it forward again. And they had to be very cautious about moving well to the side before the cannon was fired. Many a novice was killed or injured by forgetting that point during the turmoil of battle.

That was understandable when we consider just how a muzzle-loader was readied for firing. First the smoldering remains of wadding from the previous round had to be extinguished. That was done with a damp sponge at the end of a long ramrod. Sometimes a screw-device was used even earlier, because some bits of cartridge might be stuck in rough areas or flaws in the crudely cast bore.

After sponging, the vent had to be cleared with a kind of gimlet, and powder put down the muzzle, usually in a cloth bag, but sometimes just a big ladle. Then came wadding to separate powder and ball; it was oakum or yarn, ordinarily, and rammed tightly against the powder. And a man had to put one finger over the vent, or touch-hole, lest the ramming push powder into it—the wrong stuff, because lastly a very fine sort was put into the vent, unlike the corned or compressed kind under the wad.

A ball was rolled gently down the barrel, which was slightly inclined, and when against the wadding, was given three additional strikes to set it firmly in place. More wadding was shoved down on top, to keep the ball in position should there be a downward tilt of the muzzle during the battle; and then the touch-hole charged. Only then was the cannon ready to fire.

Occasionally, during a sea fight or a storm, one of the huge guns broke free, careening wildly about the deck. As the ship swayed, rose or fell to wave-action, or hogged, such a metal behemoth was terribly dangerous and destructive, and quite unpredictable. It might rush in one direction, stop suddenly, and reverse course, rolling with great speed and momentum, imperiling the crew and smashing everything in its erratic path. Hence the "loose cannon" wording.

But although well known for centuries, this kind of occurrence attained its real fame with the publication of a remarkable, underrated novel by Victor Hugo (1802-1885). This was *Ninety-Three*, a story of the last climactic year of the French Revolution. It is colorful, engrossing, and crammed with action, intrigue, suspense and larger-than-life characters, many historical. It was published in 1874, and made a considerable stir, mainly because of the loose cannon episode, which quickly became famous.

The incident occurs quite early in the novel, perhaps because Hugo uses it to establish the character of an important figure. It takes place on the frigate, *Claymore*, part of an English flotilla manned by French anti-revolutionary refugees; the force is being sent to the Vendée, that part of France most stubbornly resistant to the Revolution.

The partisans there are known as Chouans—signifying "owls"—and although very brave and determined, they have no really competent military leaders. On board the frigate, however, is a mysterious old man who has been picked by exiled counter-revolutionists to take command of the guerilla forces of the Vendée. He prefers to remain anonymous.

The ship's officers are much interested in the strange passenger, and wonder if he might be the leader so desperately needed by the Chouans. As they discuss him, Hugo ends the chapter abruptly with these pregnant words:

A frightful thing had just happened.

And then to the momentous event:

One of the carronades of the battery, a twenty-four pounder, had broken loose.

A carronade was a short, heavy, thick gun, a quasi-mortar; this one fired a ball weighing twenty-four pounds, so was clearly a massive piece. Hugo goes on, giving us a spectacular burst of description, a virtuoso performance:

This is perhaps the most frightful of all accidents at sea. Nothing more terrible can happen to a warship on the open sea and under full sail.

A cannon that breaks its moorings suddenly becomes a kind of supernatural beast. It is a machine which transforms itself into a monster. The mass speeds on its wheels, tilts when the ship rolls, plunges when it pitches, goes, comes, stops, seems to meditate, resumes its swift movement, goes from one end of the ship to the other with the speed of an arrow, spins around, slips to one side, dashes away, rears up, collides, smashes, kills, exterminates. It is a battering-ram which attacks a wall according to its own whim. Add this: the battering-ram is made of steel, the wall of wood. It is matter's entry into freedom. It is as though the eternal slave were avenging itself. It seems that the spitefulness in what we call inert objects has suddenly burst out of them, that they have lost patience and are taking a strange, obscure revenge. Nothing is more inexorable than the anger of the inanimate. That frenzied mass has the leaps of a panther, the weight of an elephant, the agility of a mouse, the stubbornness of an ox, the unexpectedness of a swelling sea, the swift blows of lightning, the deafness of the tomb. It weighs ten thousand pounds and it bounces like a child's ball. It moves in whirls abruptly cut by right angles. And what is to be done? ... You can reason with a mastiff, astonish a bull, fascinate a boa, frighten a tiger, move a lion to pity; with that monster, a cannon on the loose, there is no resource. You cannot kill it, for it is dead; and, at the same time, it is alive. It lives with a sinister life that comes to it from the infinite ... The ship, so to speak, has lightning imprisoned in its belly, trying to escape ...

It turns out that the chief gunner is responsible; he had failed to tighten the nut of the mooring chain, and carelessly shackled the four wheels of the carronade. Now, running wild, it has killed five men, and repeatedly mangled the bodies. It has also done dreadful damage to the vessel.

There are certain obvious measures to be tried. One can attempt to throw something in its path to impede its motions: a mattress, sacks of coal, coils of rope, whatever is soft and bulky. Or somebody, with dexterity and luck, might jam a pole into a wheel's spokes. There is even a small hope of slipping something under a wheel that might overturn the cannon, immobilizing it. But none of these expedients has worked. Then a figure appears, iron bar in hand; it is the guilty gunner, who after a titanic struggle full of hair's-breath escapes, succeeds in shoving the bar between the spokes. The cannon is stopped; he manages by leverage to tilt and overturn it.

Then Hugo ends the powerful scene with a tour-de-force of savage irony. The unnamed passenger turns to the panting gunner:

"Approach," he said.

The gunner stepped forward.

The old man turned to the Count du Boisberthelot, unfastened the captain's Cross of Saint-Louis and attached it to the gunner's jacket.

"Hurrah!" cried the sailors.

The marines presented arms.

The old passenger, pointing to the dazzled gunner, added, "And now, have this man shot."

The cheering was succeeded by stupefaction.

Then, in the midst of a silence like that of the tomb, the old man raised his voice. "One man's negligence has endangered this ship. At this very moment she may be lost. To be at sea is to be in the presence of the enemy ... Any mistake committed in the presence of the enemy is punishable by death. There are no repairable mistakes. Courage must be rewarded, and negligence must be punished."

When the execution is over, and a gloomy silence has enveloped the corvette, Boisberthelot points to the old man, standing thoughtfully alone, and in a soft voice says to La Vieuville, his fellow officer:

"Vendee has a leader."

These brief excerpts, which I take from a very admirable modern translation by Lowell Bair, are, to be sure, often melodramatic, but superbly done; and after Hugo's brilliant description of the tragedy, it will be difficult to see any mere human as having the blind, unpredictable destructiveness of a real loose cannon.

A Car Crash
—The "Total" Experience

In 1962, at the age of forty-seven, I learned to drive—not very well, as it turned out—and bought my first car, a new, fire-red Volvo. I knew nothing about it in any technical way; when it came to cylinders and transmissions, I was as the brutes that perish.

But a colleague at Los Angeles City College, where I taught mathematics for some years, had one, much to the wonder of other faculty members; he thought only in terms of domestic models, and often bragged about its economy and performance. It was impossible to break down, he gloated, and never needed those costly brake-jobs and tune-ups. That was good enough for me, so I spent $2,400 in cash, having no desire to pay financing charges, and being rather flushed, thanks to closing out my savings in the Teachers' Retirement Fund. I was giving up the profession in order to write full time.

That wasn't as rash a decision as it might seem. My spate of gimmicky short stories (to paraphrase Mark Twain, prose oozed from me like ottar of roses oozes from an otter!), even at a miserable three to five cents a word, was bringing in about one hundred dollars a month. And since I'd lived with bachelor frugality while teaching, investing much of my salary in fairly good mutual funds, my income, I hoped, would be adequate, at least until my writing paid better. I had the big "slicks" in mind, always remembering that *The Saturday Evening Post* paid $1,000 or more for a short story.

As to driving, I did the common, unwise thing and instead of going to a good professional connected with a school, took a few casual lessons from a laid-back friend, who in effect shoved me before the wheel of his old Pontiac, and said: OK, take over.

Actually, that was my second shot, because in 1943, a new, very callow second lieutenant in the Army, when we were moving along the Columbia River to a camp in Oregon, I conned my C.O. into letting me drive a Jeep for all of two hours. It was safe enough, with the long column inching its way bumper-to-bumper, and I pointed out that since I was teaching motor-maintenance to my battery—another typical bit of military irony, to have a guy who'd never owned a car, driven or fixed a flat, teaching kids capable of making a clunker into something ready for Indianapolis—I should at least know the gear-shift of this Army workhorse. And so I had my two hours of delight; it was a wonderful feeling and the glorious scenery added to my joy and sense of power.

As a child of the Depression, unlike today's teenagers, I didn't want, expect or hope for my own car; only rich kids had that luck, and they were scarce in 1933. My date and I used the Chicago streetcars: rickety, ancient, draughty, dirty and often jammed. Going wasn't too bad; after all, she was there, complete with the gardenia I'd bought her. But coming home was misery incarnate. The trolleys, after about ten at night, ran only every half-hour, and on weekends even less frequently. So behold me on a winter night, with the mercury near zero and the Lake Michigan wind enough to freeze a polar bear, waiting for thirty minutes or more for the two a.m. streetcar to arrive. What relief and joy finally to hear it clanging a few blocks away, and how good its fusty, but comparatively cozy, interior felt.

But back to Laguna Beach in 1962 and my real driving course. Unsure of myself for obvious reasons, having had, as a pilot might see it, no ground school at all but only flight training, I gave everything on foot—men, women, children, dogs and cats—the right of way; and the same for whatever had wheels. As my mentor remarked, with good-humored irony, I wasn't likely to be the best driver in town, but surely the most polite.

Well, after about five hours—no more, I'm sure—behind the wheel, I went in for my license exam. In any other part of the world and, in fact, in most sizable American cities, I'd have been failed on sight, but small towns are different and the DMV man who checked me out was all too tolerant. I went a few blocks, made left and right turns, and parked once—luckily a pretty good shot at that tricky maneuver. He objected only to my prissy handling of the wheel: too old-maidish. As for the written test, that, to somebody who'd taken scads of exams in college and given more, was a breeze.

And so I got my precious license on the first try, something that even bemused my teacher just a little.

I come now to the key question: why after so many years as a pedestrian, did I want or need a car? It was this Monterey area that bewitched me. While visiting here with my brother and his wife, I saw a house right on the cliffs near Hurricane Point that stole my heart; I had to buy it and live there in regal, scenic—stunningly so—isolation, writing (I hoped) voluminously and selling most of the output. It followed that I couldn't live in that location without a car, since I'd need to get all my necessities in Carmel, about seven miles away. There were not then, any more than now, trolleys on Highway 1.

And so, flushed with the valor of total ignorance, an inexperienced, not to say bad, driver, I set out for my new home, not on reasonably safe 101, but the narrow, twisting Coast Road with its scanty two lanes and terrifying heights. One goof on a turn and I could have ended up a hundred feet down in surf-battered rocks. Stacking the odds against me even more, I'd vastly overloaded the little car with all my possessions.

The only point in my favor was that I had at least reached one stage as a driver vital to progress. It's familiar to anybody who has mastered a physical skill: I no longer had to think about what to do, but just did it automatically.

Yet only a few weeks before acquiring that basic competence, I'd crashed my new Volvo in Laguna Beach. It was a shattering experience, very close to real tragedy, which could have ended my driving career for good.

I'd been having difficulty starting after a stop, so decided to get in some practice on a quiet street. It had a slight rise, just what I needed, since when stopping on such a hill, I always found the car rolling back as I tried to restart it. Coming back along the narrow, winding street, I badly misjudged my speed. The posted limit was fifteen miles an hour, but the twenty or so I was doing seemed safe and slow compared to highway traffic, which I was more used to. But, on rounding a curve, I realized too late I was wrong, and unable to turn the wheel deftly enough.

The car left the street, crossed the sidewalk, fortunately empty, rolled onto an immaculate lawn and hit a concrete planter that ran the length of a picture window. But for that solid barrier, I'd have crashed into the house's living room—and there were people in it!

It's impossible to describe my despair and horror in those few seconds that seemed to last forever. I heard metallic screeches, loud clattering and, finally, the hiss of air escaping from shredded tires. I suffered only a bruised knee, but felt both thankful and horrified on realizing I might well have driven directly into the schoolchildren a few hundred yards farther down. The owners of the house dashed out, and began berating me—justifiably; and soon the police

144

showed up. Distraught, I foolishly babbled I'd been doing only twenty, and the officer remarked dryly the limit was fifteen.

Well, my insurance company paid the whole huge bill for practically rebuilding the car, although the ink was hardly dry on the forms I'd signed when buying coverage. I still feel enormously fortunate and grateful that nobody was injured by my folly.

It was my worst and only accident, but not the last of my general foolishness as a driver. On the way to my new home, I picked up three hitchhikers (I'd not do that today, but those were more innocent times), two young women and a man, all very nice people. When I stopped for lunch—I think it was at the famous Madonna Inn, where the main attraction seems to have been the men's room, a garish spectacular in gleaming copper—it soon became clear the trio had no money to speak of, so I paid for their food. They tried to order the cheapest items, and not many of them, but I couldn't dig into my own fancier meal happily while they had cups of soup or whatever, so pressed them to join me, which they did.

And so to my final little folly as driver. In parking at the inn, I didn't notice—or forgot—that my front wheels were neatly against a typical concrete barrier, of which there was one to each space. It was about eight inches high. Well, when it came time to leave with my guests, I blithely stepped on the gas, and the car shuddered over the barrier, trapping itself, so to speak, with the concrete block between front and back wheels. Terrified that I might already have damaged something—crankcase, transmission; who knows?—I asked the man with me if he knew how to get us out of the bind. He did indeed; with the casual confidence of a born driver, not a klutz like me, he revved the engine, reflected briefly and with a judicious mixture of power and gearing, got the rear wheels over with hardly a thump.

After three years on the Coast Route, I found the perfect place for me to live—Pacific Grove. And there, deciding I no longer needed a car and glad to be rid of one, I gave it to my brother. The more I see of traffic, not to mention $20,000 cars and repair bills to match, the happier I am with that decision—and the luck of being free to make it.

And sometimes, when blocked from crossing the street by an endless snake of cars, or having to go around one in a driveway, I'm guilty of *schadenfreude*, and think of what a great boon it will be, when—not if—there is such total congestion that nothing on wheels can move and we pedestrians will again inherit the Earth!

(Not alone, warns old friend, Bradlaugh. Methinks I hear sounds of a competitor, also making a comeback after the Last Great Traffic Jam—hark! aren't those hoofbeats?)

Finding Comfort in Antisocial Security

I really only have Perfect Fun with myself. Other people won't stop and look at the things I want to look at or, if they do, they stop to please me or to humor me or to keep the peace.

—Katherine Mansfield

Having spent sixteen of my first twenty-five years in none-too-spacious apartments with my father and three brothers—my mother died when I was nine—it might be said that I had a surfeit of togetherness and didn't crave any more of it no matter how many sociologists liked the idea.

There was almost always a babble, even a roar, of conversation, none of it in the genteel, dulcet voice of a Ronald Colman; the sound of music, as one brother, a pianist, hammered away, forte, at the Grieg or Tchaikovsky concerto; that of another playing his accordion in a bedroom not even the closed door of which could muffle the wailing dissonances of that execrable excuse for an instrument, a sort of hypertrophic mouth organ; the thumps, bumps and yammerings of neighbors in other apartments in the building; and the blare of my father's Graybar radio as Hal Totten, ever enthusiastic, broadcast the Chicago Cubs' baseball game, which they rarely won. That their only first-rate pitcher, Charlie Root, one of the best in the league, never got the kind of support from his teammates he deserved, particularly irked Dad, who would mutter darkly about it.

As for me, neither a musician nor sports fan, I might be hunched over a card table, doing my homework of algebra—which completely baffled me—or a book report, much more to my taste. The noise didn't seem to bother me, but maybe my inner spirit was telling itself wistfully what bliss to be alone someday in a really quiet place. No, I was not a neutral, innocent observer but contributed my share of the din.

Well, I finally got that unspoken wish, in spades. For many years now I've not only lived alone but reveled in that lovely isolation. Let me agree, right off, that not all solitude, even to the most self-sufficient person, is pleasant. The POW kept by force in a small, dark, dank, cold—or unbearably hot—cell, badly fed, perhaps chained and physically mistreated, naturally would prefer any kind of company, even that of his worst enemy at home. And the medieval monk, alone in some chilly, lamp-lit cave with nothing whatever to occupy his mind but prayers and meditation—the first, as I see it, wasted on a mythical deity and the second with little culture to draw upon—does not stir my envy either.

But solitude in today's world is a different story. Although—and this will amaze and shock some people—I rarely speak more than a dozen sentences daily, most of them to casual listeners like the amiable folks at the library, clerks in stores or the few acquaintances I happen to meet on the streets, my total sensory input is enormous, sometimes even overwhelming. Yes, my voice, none too mellifluous at best, gets very rusty at times, so that I have to clear my throat in order to husk out a few words, but my eyes, ears and brain are flooded.

Use it or lose it, the maxim goes, but what if you don't need it?

As to the nature of that massive input, much of it is musical, mainly classical, but also that of the Big Bands, those fabulous organizations led by the likes of Duke Ellington, Benny Goodman, the Dorseys, Artie Shaw and Glenn Miller. Aided and abetted, of course, by such great sidemen as Art Tatum, Fats Waller, Earl Hines, Roy Eldridge and Lionel Hampton. And what singers they had! Frank Sinatra, Ella Fitzgerald, Anita O'Day, Sarah Vaughan, June Christy, Jo Stafford, Chris Connor, Margaret Whiting and—lest we forget!—the enchanting Ella Mae Morse, exuberantly belting out "Down the Road a Piece," backed by the great boogie piano of Freddie Slack.

Then there are radio and TV; their inputs vary from dreadful to glorious—say, from Morton Downey Jr. to *Masterpiece Theatre*—all unavailable to hermits only a century ago but now mine from which to pick and choose.

There are also, of course, books and magazines, of which I read dozens monthly. And, above all, my own creative activities, mostly writing these days, but with variants such as artwork or crazy inventions. And I write more long, gossipy letters than most people, plus some, more controversial—I expect death threats daily!—to the local newspapers.

My phone, I might add, if machines have rudimentary consciousness must feel neglected, dejected and rejected, since it's in use not more than three or four times a month on the average. (Which may be why it tried to stick me with two calls from Monterey to Germany, when I've never phoned abroad in my life.)

And so in love am I with solitude that I even discourage occasional visits from relatives dear to me, comparatively speaking—since emotionally I cast a cold eye at interpersonal relations—and although over the years many people have tried to become close, acquiring the status of friends, I've backed off, feeling guilty … but not very. I have lost all taste for small talk and no longer even care to argue religion with those Jehovah's Witnesses who keep coming, with foolish optimism, to my door.

I must ruefully plead guilty to being so involved with writing, reading and listening that I scant even basic housekeeping, and so live in a dusty, messy clutter that would send any normal person, man or woman, into shock.

Yes, I admit it, I'm a bit weird, but not too unhappy about that. To go—partway—with Shakespeare, I could be bounded in a nutshell and count myself a king of infinite space, if I have my thoughts, books and music.

Am I saying, rather brashly, that there are no drawbacks whatever in the life of a recluse? Well, almost, but not quite. There is the problem of health. If I collapsed from a coronary or stroke and could not reach the phone, I might well die here alone, since nobody would even miss me for some days—maybe weeks. But we all have to die and, in the end, no matter how many people may be at our bedsides, we're still alone, in essence, as darkness falls. And when my relations, unaccountably fond of a person completely unworthy of such affection, bring up that point and urge me to phone them if I'm stricken so they can rush over from several hundred miles away, I point out the obvious, that it makes much more sense for me to call an ambulance and head for the superbly manned Community Hospital where help that counts would be far more quickly available. I appreciate the sympathy, but a competent M.D. really fits the bill better.

Since I say so little to others, I can be excused, perhaps, for addressing myself occasionally. As with Carroll's Alice, my comments are often just good advice: "Why not get some mushrooms today for a change?" or "Say, it's been several weeks since you looked in at the St. Mary's Thrift Shop. Why not amble over?" Often, however, it's a cry of disgust over some foolishness or booboo, well laced with expletives. (As Twain wrote, "When angry, count four; when very angry, swear.") I may mutter, "You stupid &$#%$! Don't you ever learn?" Unfortunately, I usually don't and make the same mistake a few days later. But then talking to oneself is a peccadillo not entirely unknown among ordinary, gregarious people, many of whom, also like me, sometimes argue with, or grump at, the radio and TV.

Finally, I'm not alone in loving solitude; I have a lot of good company, if that's the right word. For example, Andrew Marvell:

Society is all but rude,
To this delicious solitude.

And that peerless wit and essayist, Sydney Smith:

Living a good deal alone will, I believe, correct me of my faults; for a man can do without his own approbation in society, but he must make great exertions to gain it when he lives alone. Without it, I am convinced, solitude is not to be endured.

To which Lord Byron adds, when reflecting on solitude:

It has but one disadvantage, but that is a serious one—it is apt to give one too high an opinion of one's self. In the world we are sure to be often reminded of every supposed or known defect we may have ...

I agree!

Just as they will never understand me, I'll always be puzzled by people who can't bear to be alone, even briefly, but seek out others and are happiest in big crowds. Now when I spot a Pet Parade or Good Old Days bash in Pacific Grove I go wide, skulking to my goal via the empty side streets. And when anybody asks me if I'm looking forward to some such celebration and will I be there, I smile and reply, "Not even if paid, and very well, by the hour!"

It may not be indexed for inflation or backed by all the faith and credit of the government, but I dearly cherish my own Antisocial Security!

One Man Searching for Light

When I moved to the Monterey Bay Area more years ago than I like to think about, I'd lived almost all my life in Chicago, where, oddly, despite heavy snows, gales, blizzards and wire-breaking sleet storms, we never seemed to have any power failures. At worst, as I recall, the lights might flicker ominously now and then.

I had bought a small house near Garrapata Creek, moving in at the best time of the year, when sky and ocean both smiled, and I had no idea what winter could bring. I soon learned that getting and maintaining electricity to such a place was nothing like the situation in Chicago. The poles were often set in wooded, inaccessible locations where repairs were slow and difficult. No praise would be too lavish for the gallant PG&E crews that had to fix downed wires while glacial winds blew and tremendous rains fell.

The first time my power went out, I was totally unprepared, having on hand only a few candle-stubs, which I'd brought, without even knowing why, among my possessions. Luckily, the power on this occasion was out for only two hours, just long enough to teach me a badly needed lesson. It was clear I'd better acquire some sort of emergency lighting equipment.

The first thing I learned was that candles were not the solution. They made tiny pools of light, didn't last very long and were not all that cheap. What next?

Happening to spot an ad for a gas lamp—something I'd never owned or knew beans about—I was beguiled into picking one up at a big Carmel hardware store. Although it came with directions and I bought the right fuel—white gas, I think it was called—I'd have done better to consult the clerk first. There was the matter of a tricky pump, since pressure had to be built up. After I managed that, I was disconcerted to find little leakages along the sides of the contraption; and when I lit it, the sounds were not at all reassuring. There was hissing, buzzing, whistling, little creaks and sinister pops, all of which made me tense and uneasy. Then, too, I was at least aware that gasoline is highly volatile, dangerous stuff. After a few hours over the following weeks, I gave up and retired the device for good.

And so, again, what next? A burning question, to be both literal and pun-ish.

The answer seemed obvious: get some oil lamps. They used kerosene, much safer than gas, but easy enough to keep alight, I was informed. The informer was the agent who'd sold me the house, a wise woman who had lived long in these parts. Pleased with expert advice, I got two of the big, practical lamps, not the little, decorated kind that use scented, overpriced fuel. Still the pristine naif, blissfully unaware that the Fool-Killer might be stalking me, I didn't bother to ask her for a demonstration, so one night when the power went off, I hastily set up one of the big, all-glass lamps, cranked the flat wick up by the feeble glow of a flashlight and hopefully lit it.

The results bemused me, to understate the case. A large, yellow flame appeared, looking—very briefly—bright and beautiful. Surely I could read by it, eat under its golden beams and never worry about fire, weird noises or even cost; although, to be sure, it didn't smell so good.

Then realism smashed the lovely vision. The top and sides of the flame turned jet-black and large clouds of carbon soot not only poured out of the chimney, but immediately darkened the glass to the point where the light might as well have been in a solid metal box. Now what? I wondered, frustrated and deeply puzzled. Was the fuel contaminated? The wick defective? The chimney wrongly shaped?

I extinguished the flame by rolling the wick down, and tried again. Slowly, carefully, I ratcheted up a full two inches of the absorbent fabric, struck a match and, even as my flashlight grew dim, lit the lamp. And again, for a moment, a fine, bright flame, then the relentless attack of the Soot Monster. Baffled, I gave up. Back to my reserve candles.

It wasn't until some weeks later that my friend, the real estate lady, cleared up the mystery. Nothing was wrong with fuel, lamp or wick—as she demonstrated. It was all just a strange quirk of oil lamps. She rolled up no more than a quarter inch of wick and lit it. The tiny flame was perfect and stayed so for several minutes as I held my breath. Slowly, as I stared in wonder, she ratcheted it up, so that when finally it was about an inch high, it still burned perfectly. The solution was simple once it had been explained: you had to start small and gradually extend the wick. From then on, no trouble.

I used oil lamps for years, but still longed for electricity of some sort. Flashlights and lanterns didn't work, either; in those days batteries were not as good as our modern ones. They didn't store well and when most needed were often run-down. They were expensive, too, relatively. Yes, the oil lamps were clearly adequate, but when the lights went out suddenly, often for as long as six or eight hours, I had to drag out a lamp, coax it into operation according to the immutable laws outlined above and endure its foul smell and none-too-bright illumination.

And so, revving up my imagination for an ultimate solution, I triumphed. I bought a good motorcycle-size storage battery and a trickle charger. I put them both on a big plastic tray, easily moved about for convenience, and looked for a suitable light bulb. I'd taken it for granted that only a typical 12-volt automobile bulb would be available and that I'd have to adapt it somehow. But, on a hunch, I inquired at a hardware store, learning to my delight that regular 60-watt incandescent ones, looking exactly like the regular 110-volt kind, were to be had, although a bit more expensive.

From then on, my road was clear. I put the bulb in an old desk lamp, which I easily adapted, using two clamps attached to its wiring to clip on the poles of the battery. On turning the switch, I had exactly what I wanted: a fine reading lamp available at the table for meals, as well as for newspapers, books, magazines or, for that matter, dish-washing. I recharge the battery every eight weeks or so, just topping it off, so to speak, since it gets little use, but like all its kind, loses a few percent of its charge daily even when idle.

And now, when the lights flicker out—strangely, now that I'm set, that seems to happen only rarely—I need merely to turn a switch.

There is, too, a nice added attraction, so to speak, to my storage battery and charger set-up. Not only can it be used in a blackout for excellent lighting, but also to power the 12-volt car radio I picked up for pennies at a thrift shop. And if I care to scrounge a cassette player, stereo or compact disc outfit, it will do just as well for them. It's true, of course, that there are scads of solid-state, battery-run radios around, but they have nothing like the power and endurance of a storage battery.

A cautionary note, just in case. As most car owners know, charging a battery should be done with reasonable care, since flammable gas is being produced. Obviously, both open flames, as from smoking or anything that might spark, should be avoided during the process, which is best done in a well-ventilated area.

And so, after Looking for the Light, I finally found it.

My Poisonous Pals

Who could possibly feel friendly towards a grotesque, hairy, poisonous, eight-legged little monster, which, if the size of a calf, might easily double for one of those murderous, invading alien life-forms once so common in science fiction stories?

Well, I could, and do—that's who! I respect, admire, and do indeed feel some affection towards the ugly arachnids most people know as—ugh!—spiders.

To begin with, I cite a rather cynical but psychologically plausible dictum: the enemy of my enemy is my friend. You see, I've always loathed flies. Not only are they filthy creatures, although paradoxically forever grooming themselves, but they carry a host of disease germs particularly dangerous to humans. Beyond that, I hate their buzzing, a high-pitched, wimpy noise, far worse than the shrill dive-bomb attack of mosquitoes, the somnolent, bourgeois humming of contented bees and even the harsh, menacing, but, at least, bold and feral, war-cry of an angry hornet, sounding like a miniature chainsaw in flight.

Then, too, spiders are marvelously adapted to their environments, which often overlap—to the intense annoyance of my fellow squeamish bipeds who don't share my benevolent attitude—our own. Many of them are gifted natural mathematicians. Untold eons before Euclid, the minute, pale speck of matter that comprises a spider's brain antedated some of the great geometer's best work.

156

And the web very familiar to most of us, the one shaped like a spiral, winnowed the breezes of some prehistoric summer long, long before any human being was able to write the equation of that tricky curve. Obviously, the maker of this little miracle has no degree in math, but operates by instinct, using its legs somewhat like a draftsman's dividers. The details of such a construction are fascinating, but too complicated for a brief discussion. In the appendix to his splendid book, *The Life of the Spider*, one of the ten that chronicle his life's work, the French entomologist, Jean-Henri Fabre (1823-1915)—the "insects' Homer," or, as Darwin called him, "that inimitable observer"—describes the whole process meticulously. Of course, there are many modern accounts, but none better done than that by the gifted French stylist, who wrote as well as he observed, meaning incredibly well. The actual curve is that of a logarithmic spiral, but it's only one of countless kinds of webs made by spiders. Incidentally, my reluctance to casually destroy webs in my various homes has surprised, disgusted and bemused many a friend and relation, but I've stuck to my guns: anything that efficiently kills flies is safe from me. How could I tear up the magnificent structure that cost my little uninvited guest so much labor? Without it, she could never catch a single fly, unlike many of her cousins, who have a whole armamentarium of hunting devices. Some, like the ferocious, keen-sighted wolf spiders, don't need webs; they stalk and kill a variety of insects much as a leopard goes after game in Africa—on foot, and alone. Those that do make webs are not confined to spirals: they build sheets, funnels and even underwater diving bells. Others actually lasso flying insects, and a few amazing spiders cast a net much like that of a seiner, catching their prey in flight as he does fish swimming in water.

Undoubtedly, one of the most intriguing of these webless predators is the trapdoor spider, which digs a hole in the ground, lines it with silk, and then builds a perfectly round little trapdoor, complete with a tiny hinge, and beautifully camouflaged with the same kind of soil set into a mass of the sticky threads. When an unwary insect comes by, passing near the door, the spider pops out like some monster in a typical horror film, to seize its prey. After that, which happens too fast for the eye to follow, it drops back into the burrow; the lid snaps shut, and there is no sign of the event or the den itself.

Life is replete with odd connections; in my case, between insects and symphonic music, the former leading to my interest in spiders—not insects, but close enough—and the latter to my lifelong love of classical music. It happened this way. As a boy of ten, in Chicago, I was taken to visit my bachelor uncle, a math teacher, and about as quirky as I later became myself. There, one evening, thoroughly bored with grown-up's chatter, I explored his bookcase, finding a Modern Library copy of Fabre's *The Life of the Caterpillar*. It enchanted me, especially with an account of how processionary caterpillars, which follow in each other's paths, were suckered by the French experimenter into circling the top of a large urn until exhausted, moving in a circle, with the first of the foolish critters on the trail of the last. They continued that futile round until too tired to care, falling off the urn. That magic book aroused my interest in the huge class of insects.

And on my next visit, luckily, I fooled with Uncle Will's big Victrola, and happened to put on a record of the "Unfinished Symphony" of Schubert. I was ecstatic, and from then on loved such music. Ironically, I found, my uncle knew little about, and cared less for, classical music and "bugs."

One of the puzzles about spiders that engaged Fabre, whose books I hastened to get from the library, was how they avoid getting stuck on their own webs. The stickiness, as Fabre soon learned, was caused by drops of adhesive expelled from the spider's glands; they were applied in separate beads, so that under magnification, a strand of the web looks like part of a pearl necklace.

Convinced that the spider escaped being caught because of oil on its feet, the French experimenter devised a highly ingenious means of settling that point. He took spider legs, and soaked them in a solvent, which removed all the hypothetical oil. The dry feet, he found, did indeed stick to the web. I'm not aware that any modern entomologists have either confirmed or refuted his theory, but most of them seem to think the spider simply walks on the non-sticky scaffolding strands when going out on the web after an insect. Repeating Fabre's experiment might be an interesting high school biology project.

The Baconian Fabre was not given to bizarre theories, believing only in close—very close—observations on insects in the field, but in the matter of some baby spiders, he came up with a really wild idea. The tiny infants, he noted, lived on their mother's back for many days, scrambling about very vigorously, but took no nourishment. The baffled investigator, contrary to his normal cautious bent, decided they got energy from the sun! Again, I've seen no modern reference to the phenomenon, if it exists, or Fabre's conclusion.

It should be noted that spiders do not get a free ride; nothing in nature does, although some animals like tigers and elephants have no dangerous enemies but man. Spiders have plenty, many of them killer wasps. These sting, paralyze, and bury their hapless prey, to be eaten alive by their young. Even people who detest and fear spiders might consider that a harsh fate.

Aside from aiding me to keep my house free from flies, spiders have done me two other favors, so to speak. A spider helped me launch my writing career, and a bit later, another did far better in that regard. My third published story, sold to *Boys' Life*, was the saga of a spider. Still a novice, I gave it the formal, rather square,

159

title, "The Odyssey of Epeira," which the editor immediately changed to "Eight-Legged Monster." Perhaps he was a refugee from the *National Enquirer*! That story was never reprinted, but a later one, "The Fly," which also featured one of my favorite arachnids, was a hit. After its initial appearance in *The Magazine of Fantasy and Science Fiction*, "The Fly" was reprinted at least fifteen times, and is still alive and well. It originally paid all of thirty dollars (it *was* very short), but since then has brought in, I should think, perhaps a thousand. It even had the (dubious) honor of a mild objection by Isaac Asimov, who thought no atomic reactor could fit inside a dummy fly. He may well be, and probably is, right, but I can conceive of a situation that might justify my assumption of a small fission device, one that instead of requiring a sizeable lump of uranium isotope, might utilize a laser beam impinging on a pellet of U-235, as is being done now with attempts at fusion by laser and deuterium. This set-up, clearly, could be fitted into a tiny space.

Since I came to Pacific Grove decades ago, my poisonous little cronies, alas, have fallen upon hard times. Unlike Chicago, where, as a boy, I saw more insects of all kinds—grasshoppers, bluebottles, crickets, ants, bees, wasps, mantids and caterpillars—in any weedy vacant lot than there are in the whole state of California these days, for some reason, maybe the cool, foggy climate, there are relatively few insects here, even though my house would send any self-respecting pig into catatonic shock. I rarely have a fly in the place, partly because I try hard to shut them out, no matter what route they attempt; so my few remaining spiders must subsist, as nearly as I can figure out, on a diet of fluffy, insubstantial clothes moths. Even they are scarce, since my scanty, decrepit wardrobe offers them little sustenance.

So I think wistfully of the time long ago, a warm summer night in Chicago, when I was feverishly working at my old Royal to finish a story before having to leave to teach a night-school math course at

De Paul University. Suddenly, from nowhere—at night, too, which is not typical of the vile species—appeared a huge fly, the size of a helicopter gunship, it seemed, and almost as noisy. It was impossible to write while it zoomed and buzzed about the room and even my aching head. Furious, I pursued it with a rolled-up newspaper, but in vain; it flew too high, and, as we now know, has the kind of vision that makes for superb dodging. It seemed to buzz in derision. My swearing had just reached an incandescent crescendo, when suddenly there was silence, followed by a shriller, panicky sound. The pest had sailed squarely into a newly built spiral at a corner of the room near the ceiling. What a relief! I rejoiced.

I promptly returned to the typewriter. Although I didn't watch the inevitable outcome, being no lover of nature's cruelties, I knew very well what she—it's almost always a female in at the death; males are good only for reproduction—was up to. Most of the web spinners are cautious, even cowardly, executioners. She would move over the surface—unstuck!—to the victim, but pause a safe distance away, even though a fly is totally defenseless, having neither sting nor fangs, unlike other occasional prey, such as bees or wasps. Once close, she would turn her back, and, from those remarkable spinnerets that provided material for her web, cast sheets of silk over the fly, which she then manipulated with her hind legs, rolling it into a helpless mummy, unable to move, clad, veritably in a shroud. A quiet killing, of course, the trapper being mute, like most of her species, the only sound a muffled fizzing from the doomed insect. That would not last long, either, because now the timid spider, aware that her prey was completely immobilized, would glide in, and with two hollow fangs like those of a tiny rattlesnake, inject the potent venom that kills so quickly.

And as I finished my story in peace, she enjoyed her dinner, perhaps even listening, along with me, to music from the radio. It should have been, if the cosmos were informed by a demiurge with

161

a flair for quirky, black humor, Albert Roussel's "The Spider's Feast," but was, actually—speak, memory!—the limpid elegance of "Rosamunde," by Franz Schubert.

And, until my tiny friend mysteriously vanished a few months later, that's exactly what I named her—Rosamunde.

Lessons Learned
From a Pair of Cats

At one time, years ago in Laguna Beach, I owned—or was tyrannized over by—two young cats, illogically named, since they were brothers, Gilbert and Sullivan. The latter may have been part Manx, since he had only a stub of a tail.

The naming of pets, I hasten to add, mostly dogs and cats in this country, shows a deplorable lack of imagination. I've known too many people who called their pets Tabby, Fluffy, Blackie and similar overused, unevocative names. There are dozens of better ones available from literature and music, to name only two fields ripe for gleaning. Why not Zerlina, Sancho Panza, Pickwick or Beckmesser?

In any case, I had these two cats and like many a pet owner was concerned with their welfare. Early on, I tired of letting them in and out, and decided to design a small swinging panel at the bottom of the kitchen door. I made it about a foot square, snugly fitted at the edges to keep out mice and even flies; and to stop it from being too easily flapped about by breezes, I used a small but powerful magnet on one side. When the little door was properly aligned in the shut position, the magnet was attracted to a metal pin, holding the door firmly closed. The magnet did not touch the pin—that would have made the panel too hard for my cats to open—but merely attracted it from about one-tenth of an inch away. Thus a firm push by a cat's nose would break the attraction.

At that point in my project, I learned an interesting bit of cat psychology that was new to me. It is this: a cat is too cautious a beastie to nose through any panel blindly; it has to see what's on the other side, or no deal. Gilbert and Sullivan would not use the door until I fitted a bit of screen over a hole in the center, allowing them to peek out into the yard or into the kitchen before swinging the little door.

Something else I learned from Sullivan relates to the old puzzle of just how a cat manages always to land on its feet, even if turned upside down and dropped (on something soft, I hasten to add, lest the SPCA send a hit man!) from a height of only two or three feet. This feat seems to some to violate a law of physics, the one involving conservation of angular momentum. Some scientists have thought a cat accomplishes the trick by using its tail, which when rotated counter to the turning of its body allows for the seeming anomaly without any violation of the basic law.

Well, all I can say is that Sullivan, with only a stub, and no long, wavy appendage like Gilbert's, still never failed to land on his feet. As T. H. Huxley would have wryly noted, another beautiful theory slain by an ugly fact.

As for the little door, I was baffled for weeks by my cats' refusal to use it; surely they were intelligent enough to master the trick. I'd always felt cats were not only as bright as dogs, but much more independent, and so admirable. What was wrong with these dummies? Had I acquired a mentally retarded pair of siblings?

As noted, the screen cleared up the problem. The cats were plenty smart enough to use the door, but too smart to shove themselves blindly into anything. Once they could see, the panel was swinging constantly—more, in fact, than I cared for. The constant to-ing and fro-ing annoyed me, especially late at night when I was trying to sleep.

And unlike dogs, cats don't give a damn about their "owner's" opinions. A dog, if yelled at for something a few times, will usually change its ways, but no cat ever altered its behavior out of deference to the simpleton who mistakenly felt in authority over the critter.

I learned many things about the feline psyche during my three years with Gilbert and Sullivan. For example (again in contrast with dogs, who are greedy and gluttonous enough not merely to overeat whenever given the chance, but never get tired of any food they tolerate at all), cats are as finicky as most humans: in short, they get bored with any victuals, even top grade tuna or crêpes suzette. And perversely, for some obscure reason, a cat will suddenly abandon a favorite dish of its own in order to take a few scruffy morsels from its owner's plate.

Getting back to the door (and while building it, I couldn't help thinking of one of my two all-time cat jokes, about the man who had not one, but two cat panels in his front door, one bigger than the other. When asked about this, he pointed out that he had an adult cat and several kittens, adding, "When I say 'scat!' I mean 'scat!' " The other joke, I add for completeness, also serves as my answer to the frequent question, "Do you like cats?" to which I reply, smirking: "Oh, he's okay, but I really go for Mrs. Katz!"), it lasted and functioned for only a few weeks. One night, I awoke to a terrible racket: clattering noises, caterwauling, spitting and a mad yowling came from the kitchen. When I investigated, I realized that two strange toms, as bright as my own pets—and a lot more aggressive, bullies both—had chased them into the house and, with never a qualm, invaded my property as if invulnerable. Well, like the fellow in my joke, I yelled, "scat!" in a stentorian voice, and all four fled in terror.

But I knew the swinging panel had suddenly become obsolete. The next morning I locked it for good. From then on, Gilbert and Sullivan came and went only when I was ready, willing and able to play doorkeeper.

Relating the Strange
Story of a Story

In 1967, after about fifty years of city living, mostly in apartments, I found myself alone in a rural, not to say wild, setting near Garrapata Creek. Early on, my initiation had begun with the killing of a rattlesnake, the first I'd ever met outside of a book. I heard its warning, more like a buzz than a rattle, and although the sinister sound was new to me, recognized it at once, and grabbed a hoe that was handy. I murdered the baby reptile, only about a foot long at most, and immediately regretted that wanton act. It had only warned me to keep clear, as it had a right to do. I never attacked one again, having no natural fear or dislike of snakes, but a biologist's approval of their role, generally helpful to man.

I'd bought a cottage, where following many tribulations with a cranky wood stove, my only source of heat, I ordered an oil burner from Sears, one designed to be free-standing, requiring only a vent pipe to the outside. Like almost everything supposed to be easily assembled, it wasn't quite, except maybe for a full professor of mechanical engineering; but I finally had it ready to go. Only then did I notice some minuscule print, which sternly cautioned me to place the boxy contraption on a fireproof base, or else.

Comes now an unlikely combination of asbestos-board, a small car and *Silybum*—the latter, not as might seem the case, a British obscenity, but a very nasty weed. The odd trio led to the writing of one of my best stories, and certainly the highest paid.

Until then, I'd been turning out reams of stuff for from two to five cents a word, mostly to detective and science fiction magazines. Since I was primarily the creator of ingenious gimmicks, devoting little time to either character or description, the stories were quite short, seldom more than 2,000 words, so my take for each was not exactly a matter of high finance. And just over the literary horizon, beckoning invitingly, were the big "slicks," as they were known to us ink-stained wretches, led by *The Saturday Evening Post*, with *Collier's* and *Good Housekeeping* also in the van. They planked down from $2,000 and up—way up—for a short story. I had the minimal good sense to know that my gimmicky little tales would never go over at such places, so didn't even bother to nag my agent. It was enough, on the whole, that I'd sold over 200 of them to the likes of *Alfred Hitchcock's Mystery Magazine*, *Ellery Queen's Mystery Magazine* and *The Magazine of Fantasy and Science Fiction*. It also helped that a number had been reprinted and even anthologized in prestigious collections. I'd even appeared in one such volume with C. S. Forester and Hemingway; not much money, but a dash of glory, good enough for me. And at least two of mine outperformed most of theirs in one way, at least—"The Ruum" and "The Fly" (no, not the famous one, made into two movies so far), both science fiction, have been reprinted, here and abroad, over forty times between them, and in many foreign languages, besides being dramatized for radio. Not that I'm about to tempt the Fool-Killer again by equating numbers and popularity with literary merit; I'm well aware that Harold Robbins sells more books in a week than Robert Graves did in his best decade.

However, back to the strange trio and what they wrought. Cold weather was imminent, and I was anxious to make the heater operational as soon as possible, so drove to Carmel, the nearest town, for the asbestos-board. Having decided, with the builders' supply shop owner's help, on a four-by-six foot slab, we found it would not fit anywhere inside the Volvo. After some cogitation by both of us, and the rejection of various impracticable solutions, he suggested we tie it to the roof, which we did. But when I was inside, and ready to drive off, we found the sheet to be rather wobbly, so he used more thin, strong wire to fasten it to both door-handles. Then, satisfied the board would stay in place at least until I got home, I left.

Once back at my house, I tried to get out of the car, only to find both doors wired shut. It was just a minor annoyance, since, after some vigorous tugging, I got one open, and squeezed out; but as I freed the asbestos-board, inspiration struck. What if somebody was so thoroughly wired in, they could not get out? Even if the victim managed to lower a window, it's difficult, maybe impossible, to break tough wire—say, piano wire—without cutters, and who carries those routinely in a car? Aha! The idea was building up.

What could be the circumstances, and whom for the driver? Obviously, if a person were trapped that way on some reasonably well traveled highway, they'd soon be rescued by the Highway Patrol or some passing motorist. So I had to think of a convincing scenario to prevent that possibility. And for a suitable victim, somebody particularly helpless, pitiable: a small, frail woman, say; an amputee, paraplegic.

Well, I thought about it on and off for several days, and the various pieces began to fit seamlessly. The driver would be a salesman, a rather nerdish type; that would do, and explain his route, too. But to turn the screw further, he must be in a great hurry to get back home, so that finding himself delayed, wired in, would be truly devastating. Ah! He's hurrying home because his beloved little daughter, he's just learned by a telegram from his wife, is dying of leukemia, with only days to live.

So cramming his rather schlock merchandise—cheap ties, say—in the car, he drives off … no, that wouldn't do; gives the gimmick away far too soon; no suspense or mystery. After further reflection, the answer came with complete conviction. A few months earlier I'd read a splendid short story by Daphne du Maurier; it was called "No Motive," and began with a mysterious suicide that seemed to be totally without reason. I'd steal from her—what better source?—that angle, and begin with the finding of a man's skeleton in an old, rusty, beat-up car.

But how could such a car remain undiscovered for years? Even on some back road, that was very unlikely. The problem stumped me for days, until I happened to be chopping away with a grass whip at some weeds—terrible stuff, with incredible needles. A friend told me it was milk thistle, a member of the *Silybum* genus. Well, I thought, swinging viciously at the clump, if a lot of that grew up around an old car, nobody would poke around casually in such stuff!

Still, that wasn't the whole solution; more was needed. Then I got the final inspiration. The salesman, one Kolitz, would be racing home all right, but just after he left, the Japanese attacked Pearl Harbor. In the excitement, even panic, that followed, everything was disrupted. There was no gas for casual driving; the back roads were little used; people were preoccupied with vital matters, so a car might well be unnoticed long enough for *Silybum*, other weeds, even snow, to blur and hide it from very infrequent travelers.

All I needed now was the actual wiring. Why would anybody do such a thing to an innocent, hapless salesman? There were many possibilities, but only one I could use. If my story was to open with a seemingly pointless, unmotivated suicide, the wirer had to be essentially innocent himself. Make him a young kid—no, two of them; a friend witnesses him doing it—who on the way home from a private prep school, finds a spool of piano wire dropped by some defense company's truck, and spotting Kolitz's car, with him asleep inside, decides to play a little joke—wire the guy in. Caught up in war-hysteria, he and his schoolmate don't go back.

The salesman, exhausted in his long, high-speed drive back to California, has pulled off for a nap. An accident on the main highway has forced him to detour, since he can't afford any delay with his child dying. So the kid quietly wires him in, doing a very thorough job, wrapping one coil after another around, over, and through, with knots, loops, and tangles until it looks like a fish net. My blood chilled as I visualized the denouement: the harried Kolitz, weary, strung-out, a rather flabby man with bad feet, awakening from his unrestful nap, is unable to get out of the immobile car, and perishes, never to reach his daughter or wife, who doesn't know what happened to him, and won't for decades. All was clear to me now. I'd open with the totally mysterious suicide of a man who has everything: health, a loving, beautiful wife, a fine career, many friends—and why not? He's a wonderful guy, kind, generous, sensitive and with a clear conscience. So why would he suddenly kill himself? The answer turned out to be obvious: made aware, long after the fact, about how his boyish prank has led to a terrible tragedy, he can't bear the guilt.

For once I was determined to go beyond the gimmick, great as I felt it to be. I would develop character and pad the story out as much as possible, all of which I did. Then, for the first time, full of enthusiasm and hope, I told my agent to try it on some "slicks"— talk about audacity! But, much to my gratification, he agreed, feeling the story was indeed unusual. He was, I might note in passing, Scott Meredith, just starting out then, but now, as many know, one of the biggest around, with clients like Richard Nixon and million-dollar contracts almost daily.

The rest is quickly told. Ordinarily it took two or three weeks, at least, to sell a story, but in this case, Scott called me back in just a few days with the wonderful news that *Cosmopolitan* loved "The Reason," and was buying it for $1,000. I was, of course, ecstatic, although tempering my enthusiasm with the sobering thought that I'd never get such a good idea again.

There is, however, a less pleasant coda, alas. At that very moment of triumph, *Cosmopolitan* changed both editors and format, going in for sex and beauty—the new editor, Helen Gurley Brown, had previously written the bestselling book, *Sex and the Single Girl*—which meant that this type of suspense-mystery story was no longer of interest. Brown generously let me keep the money (I suppose that, legally, she could not have reclaimed it, but was charmingly gracious, I must say) but the story was not published there. Meredith tried it next on *Cavalier*, a top magazine for men, which bought it immediately, this time for a mere—not so; that was still big bucks to me then!—$400, printing the story in their July 1967 issue as "The False Face." And since that sale, "The Reason" (under its original title) has been anthologized several times, most recently in the two-volume *A Treasury of Great Mysteries*, published in 1973 by Doubleday. It would make an excellent one-off TV drama, but I've never held my breath!

And so that's the strange story of a story. It's not actually my own favorite, but surely ranks in the top five. Maybe some day, say in 2030, an essayist, writing for *Weekend* magazine, will call it a story that bites!

Love, Death and Mystery

This must be the most bizarre, incredibly poignant love story ever recorded. Many will insist that it could never have happened, is obviously impossible, and a matter of pure fantasy from some over-imaginative storyteller. Yet it's written down, very objectively, even coldly, which wasn't easy for the author, as you'll see.

He was a famous—although almost unknown to the public of his time, a typical necessity for his profession—British spy, Walter Tillman Clarke, active at the peak of his career during the French Revolution. A tall, extremely handsome, stalwart young man, he was a distinguished graduate of Oxford, and, of course, a patriot. He spoke flawless French, and had scores of friends in Paris, where he was accepted as a stereotypical aristocrat with little on his mind but horses, women and gambling.

His small, tattered notebook, long thought lost or buried forever in the British Secret Service archives, was recently discovered in the attic of a big, Elizabethan house. It was hidden by pounds of trivial papers, books and hundreds of copies of *Punch*, left there by a descendant who died last year. In it there is recorded in Clarke's minute, but legible script, the whole tragic story. It was he, I should note, who told his superiors that the revolting Jean-Paul Marat, one of the most fanatical and brutal of all the revolutionaries, was almost certainly about to be assassinated. As any historian of the period knows, he was indeed fatally stabbed in his bath, where he soaked himself often to control a disfiguring skin disease, one that some felt mirrored the foul corruption of his soul, by Charlotte Corday, who had vowed to kill either him or his master, Robespierre. She picked Marat after he declared his intention to execute 200,000 more "aristocrats," more than the country had, in fact. Just as, lying in his bath, he cried, "I'll have them all guillotined in Paris!" she stabbed him to the heart.

It's said that Clarke also informed the British Secretary of State that Robespierre's implacable foe, Georges Danton, the moderate, lionhearted member of the Committee of Public Safety, later dominated by his enemy, was going to be arrested and almost certainly guillotined.

His best contact in gathering intelligence data was a lovely young—she was only nineteen—woman named Solange Messager. As a distant relative of the firebrand, Madame Roland, the one who declaimed, "O Liberty, what crimes are committed in thy name!" she had access to many leaders of the Revolution, especially Robespierre, the cold, calculating, subtle "Incorruptible," who looked like the lawyer he was, but had the character of a modern serial killer.

The tall, fearless young Englishman joined forces with the French girl, whose façade of sweet provincial innocence perfectly concealed a keen intellect and her unquenchable hatred for the extremists who had taken over her beloved country, especially Robespierre, whose cold-blooded, legalistic tactics masked a desire for endless numbers of executions, and his chief supporter, the cryptic, strange, ideologue, Saint-Just, handsome as a god, but without a scintilla of compassion.

It was inevitable that these two young people should fall in love, but the depth of their mutual devotion was immeasurable, to judge from the outcome, which also has the air of a mystery, a controversy about human physiology still unresolved more than two centuries after their tragic, short-lived romance. It poses the old question: can such things be?

It was easy enough for them to meet, since she was an unattached young woman at a time when the social and family mores were in complete disrepair, and there was nobody to question her morals; and he, as noted, passed as an aristocratic British playboy, although that term was probably not used then.

She had been trained as a seamstress, and by making some dresses for relations of Robespierre, had won his confidence enough so that occasionally he allowed her to tidy up his messy office. There was, luckily, no hanky-panky, since it seems that the dictator was a close-to-asexual man, who lived only for politics and conspiracy. What would have happened, considering Clarke's courage, if Robespierre had tried to seduce Solange, is problematical, but I suspect the spy would have killed the fanatic and taken the consequences.

But it never came to that; the end was actually worse in most respects. After the two lovers had enjoyed their relationship for several months, Robespierre came home unexpectedly early from the Legislative Assembly to find Solange rummaging among his papers, and obviously not just to tidy them. The upshot was inevitable; betrayal was bad enough, but spying for the despised aristocrats was unforgivable. The young woman was quickly tried, the usual travesty of the times, and sentenced to death. On learning of this, Clarke nearly went mad. He tried soliciting some of his most influential friends, but in vain; the crime was too blatant, Robespierre's fury too great; nothing could be done.

I come now to the final, deeply tragic, entry in Clarke's notebook. He didn't want to be present at the execution—would anybody in such circumstances?—but he had not been permitted, despite all his pleas, dangerous enough for somebody in his profession, and the importuning of both officials and friends, to visit

Solange in prison, so this would be his last chance to see her. He writes:

As the tumbrel, with its closely packed, pathetic victims, almost all innocent, I knew, drew near, my rage and despair became unbearable. I strove desperately for a glimpse of her. Finally I did see her, noting with a kind of dazed relief that she seemed resigned, even tranquil. Our eyes met very briefly, and her face became radiant, but then the mob, fighting for places near the guillotine, jostled me aside, and I lost contact.

But I was determined to see it to the end, and used all my strength to break through the hostile crowd, which included many women, and not well nourished in these terrible times, so hardly strong enough to stop me. I found a spot near the basket, a bloody, horrible thing, but I hardened my resolve and persisted.

The end came quickly enough; poor Solange, apparently anxious to get it over with, pressed to the front. The monsters strapped her down; she made no resistance; raised the dreadful blade, and as I started to sob, prepared to drop it. I felt a nearly intolerable urge to denounce the Revolution and join her in death, but realized it was now too late for that; my guillotining would in that case not be immediate, but after days, at least.

Then the mob roared its insatiable demand for more blood, and the sharp steel fell. Whatever is charged against the guillotine, it's fast and sure— Solange's head dropped into the basket only inches from me. And now the incredible happened, or did I dream it on that awful morning just a week ago? Her wonderful blue eyes, always so full of life, opened, meeting mine squarely with obvious awareness, and her lips moved, soundlessly, of course, saying—I swear it!—"I love you, Walter." Then her eyes closed forever ...

As owner of the notebook, what can I add? Only that there is some evidence, scanty, vague and inconclusive, that consciousness may indeed persist for some seconds after a beheading. It's just one more mystery about the human brain, that enormously complex organ, the final secrets of which still elude us so long after the death of Clarke's beloved.

Not Necessarily the Britannica

The joys of fiction—novels, short stories—and poetry have often been celebrated. Few among us have had no experience at all of at least one of the three varieties; even people who brag about not having read a book in years, will admit, if grudgingly, that as children they liked *The Tale of Peter Rabbit* or *Treasure Island*.

Equally familiar as a source of pleasure are the many categories of nonfiction: essays, biographies, histories and true adventures, to name only a few; the list is long.

But there is another delight of words, a sort of orphan subclass of nonfiction, that satisfies some of us in the same way that crusty, home-baked bread and rich, thick soup are more acceptable in the long run than caviar and truffles. I refer to the huge and various group of reference books. Not the well known, thoroughly publicized ones, the bestselling, multi-volumed encyclopedias, or even the distinguished *Oxford English Dictionary*, but their offbeat, quirky, poor relations.

One of the oldest of these, and perhaps the best, is before me now. It first appeared in 1868, but my edition, the third, is undated; probably it was printed about 1872. It contains almost 1,000 pages of very small type, and has these intriguing, inviting words on the title page:

DICTIONARY
OF
PHRASE AND FABLE
giving the
Derivation, Source, or Origin of Common Phrases, Allusions
and Words that have a Tale to Tell.
BY THE REV.
E. COBHAM BREWER, LL.D.

That sixth line, as Twain might have said, will fetch most of us! It is impossible to give more than a hint of the richness inside this fat quarto-size volume dressed in faded red, but where else could one find almost three columns listing giants—from mythology, fiction and history? One of these, quite irresistible, is Angoulaffre of the Broken Teeth, who was:

Twelve cubits in height, his face measured three feet across, his nose was nine inches long, his arms and legs were each six feet, his fingers six inches and two lines ... He was descended from Goliath ... He had the strength of thirty men ... Some say the Tower of Pisa lost its perpendicularity by the weight of Angoulaffre, who one day leaned against it to rest himself.

After that, the real giants, found in records, seem pretty tame, like:

Cotter (Patrick), the Irish giant, died 1806. Height eight feet seven and a half inches ...

Brewer notes at the end of his list that:

No known specimen of man has reached the height of nine feet.

The book is crammed with other fascinating summaries, like one detailing all the famous swords of literature and history, and another on horses. Most literate people know Excalibur, Arthur's sword,

178

pulled from the stone, but who can name that of Charlemagne, which was Joyeuse; or Mohammed's scimitar, Al-Battar (the beater)? Thirty-five of the weapons are given.

As to horses, the name Pegasus is familiar, but what about Hector's steed, named Podarge, meaning "swift-footed"? Four columns, with at least sixty horses, are devoted to the subject.

For some reason, Brewer begins his dictionary with a brief account entitled:

CURIOUS LITERARY BLUNDERS.

He includes the mention of turkeys in Shakespeare's *Henry IV*, since they come from America, not even discovered for a century after that king reigned; and faults the Irish poet Thomas Moore for writing the lovely couplet:

As the sun-flower turns on her god, when he sets,
The same look which she turn'd when he rose!

It is, of course, from "Believe Me, If All Those Endearing Young Charms," and Brewer denies the flower was named because of its sun-worshipping contortions, but because he felt it resembled a picture sun. Other references I have confirm this view.

A somewhat similar compendium, also wearing red, is undated too, and looks contemporary (although I understand it was first published in 1900). It is much shorter, but has a title page more crowded; a spatter of fruity, expansive nineteenth-century prose:

THE NUTTALL ENCYCLOPEDIA
being a
Concise and Comprehensive Dictionary of General Knowledge
consisting of
over 16,000 Terse and Original Articles on nearly all subjects
discussed in larger Encyclopedias, and specially dealing

with such as comes under the categories of
History, Biography, Geography, Literature,
Philosophy, Religion,
Science and Art.
EDITED BY THE
REV. JAMES WOOD.

There is even more, but I'll spare you the rest, part of which is the puzzling information that the book was published in Japan. This chunky volume of only 700 double-column pages is not just in small print, but so tiny one suspects it was set up by one of those specialists in the minute who engrave the heads of pins. Both of these books are splendid for browsing, but *The Nuttall Encyclopedia* is far more factual, so somewhat less fun.

More restricted as to subject matter, but still vast otherwise, are the two huge volumes, 10" x 7" x 3", each over 1,200 pages, double-column, that comprise the information indicated by the title page:

UNIVERSAL PRONOUNCING DICTIONARY
OF
BIOGRAPHY
AND
MYTHOLOGY
BY
JOSEPH THOMAS, M.D., LL.D.

As you see, it offers something the other two do not—how to pronounce all those tricky names: German, French, Latin, Greek, even Arabic, but is lacking on science and history. Still, a magnificent pair, dating from 1905. It has some excellent engravings of famous people, too; the other references have no illustrations at all. One of these is of Thomas Jefferson, for example, and gives him three-and-a-half columns of very small print, much better coverage than in Wood's *The Nuttall Encyclopedia*, which has a short paragraph, and Brewer's *Dictionary of Phrase and Fable*, which has nothing whatever.

Much more specialized, and less long in the tooth, is *The Cyclopedia of World Authors*, edited by Frank N. Magill. It's dated 1958, and has 1,000 double-column pages, which is surprising, since the book seems only a bit larger than a normal 1986 novel. It devotes a page, on the average, to each author; more to the giants like Dickens, Cervantes, Shakespeare, Goethe and such. The first entry deals with Pierre Abélard; the last, Arnold Zweig. The first is well known by name, but little read, I suspect; the latter was once fairly popular—he wrote the bitter and realistic *The Case of Sergeant Grischa*, a war novel in the same mood as Remarque's *All Quiet on the Western Front*—but is now largely forgotten. A very useful reference, but obviously not as much pure fun as the others mentioned.

Another book, even more specialized, is also a collector's item in the field of science fiction. It is *Pilgrims Through Space and Time*, compiled by J. O. Bailey. Subtitled *Trends and Patterns in Scientific and Utopian Fiction*, it is all that, to be sure, but its modest 321 pages also list hundreds of classic books in the field, with brief synopses of their plots. It was published in 1947, and a mint copy is worth about twenty dollars.

If you really want specialization, consider the next two references, one fairly old, dating from 1922, the other quite recent, having appeared in 1973. Neither has any text to speak of, something not usually associated with the genre. The first consists entirely of military maps; it is *American Campaigns*, by Matthew Forney Steele, a major in the Second United States Cavalry—yes, we still had one then!—and in 305 pages it shows the terrain and tactics of all this country's battles, from the Revolutionary War to the one with Spain. Frankly, I can't say it has ever riveted my attention. The newer volume is *An Atlas of Fantasy*. It also has maps, but of the imagination: there is one covering Stevenson's *Treasure Island*; Burroughs' "Barsoom" (Mars); Cabell's imaginary "Poictesme"; Faulkner's "Yoknapatawpha" county; and a host of others almost unknown even to avid readers in the field, like Verne's "Chairman Island," "Babyland" and Leiber's "Lankhmar in the Land of Nehwon." It was compiled by J. B. Post and is great fun to leaf through.

If it's dates you want—not when Madonna was born, or Pet Rocks invented—but important, significant historical ones, you'll relish *An Encyclopedia of World History*, which has them in droves, from Paleolithic times—so help me!—to 1946, when the 1940 edition was revised, prior to its republication in 1948. It also has remarkable genealogical tables for every royal family known, however minor or ruling whatever tiny principality centuries ago. It was compiled by William L. Langer, and has 1,171 pages of minuscule type. If you want to know when the Treaty of Guadalupe Hidalgo, which certified our highway robbery of Mexico, bringing us California as booty, was signed, or when Rome was first sacked, this is the reference to own. It also has dozens of useful maps.

If you are seriously interested in music, as ever more people are of late, you simply must acquire a superb paperback put out by the wonderful folks at Dover Publications; it is *Music for the Piano*, by James Friskin and Irwin Freundlich. This unique book has almost everything of importance in the literature; for example, it covers thirty of Beethoven's thirty-two sonatas, analyzing, though briefly, the individual movements, and even indicating their difficulty of performance. Similarly, you will find just about everything Chopin ever wrote for the piano: études, mazurkas, waltzes, ballades and sonatas, each carefully explored and evaluated. No important composers, and few of the minor ones, are overlooked; and later on, duets and piano four-hands works are similarly treated, after which the authors discuss all the major concertos. A magnificent reference! Whenever I listen to our fine local station, KBOQ, I keep it handy.

And finally, considering the non-stop increases in medical costs, there are those books that help one decide intelligently which symptom, if any, ought to be taken seriously, or whether the greatest, cheapest of all physicians, Dr. Time, can handle your case. The best known and most popular of these is the small but comprehensive *The Merck Manual*, which has been compiled by various editors down the years. It has over 1,900 pages of tiny print that cover almost every disease or disability likely to afflict us. For each it goes into the symptoms, prognosis and treatment. You find, predictably, a great many entries dealing with headaches and digestive troubles, both very common, and few on Elephant Man's Disease, or pheochromocytoma. If you scan it too often, visions of rare, horrible ailments can occur, but after a while, most readers learn to relax. The book also has material on drugs, both prescription and over-the-counter, and even on diets: bland, low-sodium; low fat; and many others.

Much as I admire *The Merck Manual*, I rather prefer *Symptoms: The Complete Home Medical Encyclopedia*, by Sigmund S. Miller. It's a bit less technical, and, as the title indicates, concentrates on symptoms, and so is easier to work with. After identifying your terminal ailment, you can then get to *The Merck Manual*! But it is really useful for eliminating pointless fears. If you think you suffer from Dutch Elm Disease, for example, you will soon discover that an excessive fondness for sardine malts doesn't apply. Seriously, however, if either of these references saves you a fifty-dollar visit to the doctor—and I have been saved many such—they are fine investments. It should be noted, in conclusion, that a good medical dictionary, with plenty of clear illustrations—muscles, nerves, bones, glands, the works—is also a great book to have around. My best (I have several) is the huge *The American Illustrated Medical Dictionary*, edited by W. A. Newman Dorland. It's an oldish edition, but ninety percent of the material still seems to apply. And there are almost 1,600 double-column pages of it!

Confessions of a Biblioneurotic

If I were charged with being an habitual, incorrigible bibliomaniac, I would indignantly declare my complete innocence, but might be plea-bargained down to admitting occasional misdemeanors in bookstores. You could, so to speak, call me a biblioneurotic.

There was a time, to be sure, when I verged on true madness; then I naively dreamed about finding a mint copy of *Tamerlane and Other Poems*. It would be in a huge, musty, dusty, jam-packed old place, with volumes on shelves, tables, chairs, stools, in cupboards and on all three floors of the building. This establishment—and, believe me, there once were several such in Los Angeles—would be owned and managed, of course, by an ignorant, purblind, bored dealer, who had just inherited the business from, say, an uncle, recently deceased. Unlike the late expert, the nephew would be as the brutes that perish about first editions and incunabula—that is, books published before 1500.

The little pamphlet would be in a worthless old tome, say a collection of dull, prosy sermons by an obscure, long-forgotten divine, published about 1820. Moved by some vagrant impulse or wonderful inspiration, I would idly pick it up from a rickety table in some dark corner, and riffle the pages. Then, the shattering epiphany—the booklet! I would stare at the title page, reading:

TAMERLANE AND OTHER POEMS
BY A BOSTONIAN
Young heads are giddy, and young hearts are warm,
And make mistakes for manhood to reform.—Cowper
CALVIN F. S. THOMAS ... PRINTER
BOSTON: 1827

Published in an edition of 500, of which only about seven are now thought to exist, it is a true rara avis among books. It was valued at $25,000 fifty years ago, and now? Well, some dealers shrug, and say, "Anything you ask." The Bostonian, of course, was Edgar Allan Poe, a first edition of whose two-story pamphlet *The Murders in the Rue Morgue* (the title story was originally published in *Graham's Magazine*) would be almost as great a find. (I could add, at this point, don't bother to look for either. Why waste your time? But then, why should I kill some other novice's dream?)

But back to my mad vision. I would peer about the shadowy store, terrified that the owner had spotted my discovery and excitement. Then I'd hastily slip the pamphlet back into the fat collection of sermons. No—I must not; I cannot. I wasn't reared so; it would be stealing. What *is* permitted to book-hunters? Well, I needn't tell the dealer all about *Tamerlane and Other Poems*; it's his business to know. I can bring him the booklet, and say, disingenuously, something like: "What're you asking for this little old book of verses? They're anonymous, and pretty amateurish, but I kinda like 'em." The fellow would peer nearsightedly in the bad light, and, mind on other matters, say, "How about fifty cents?"

Well, a few such dreams have come true for some collectors, but not for me. And I'm no longer a bibliomaniac, but still have more modest dreams, and have indeed made a few nice finds. The very first rare book I ever owned, however, still on my shelf, was a gift, given to me on my graduation from college by a friendly English professor. It is a first edition of Mark Twain's *Following the*

Equator. Not his most celebrated work, but very readable, if shamelessly padded with historical data "lifted" by the author from other books. The thick, heavy volume, bound in blue, came out in 1897. I still thank you, Professor Mollie Cohen, for the thoughtful present.

The first rare book I acquired on my own was new and cheap when I bought it. I was browsing in a Los Angeles store, and picked up a thin volume of short stories entitled *Dark Carnival*. The page I happened to scan had a veritable burst of brilliant description, and obviously dealt with matters I already adored—wild, imaginative, fresh fantasy. Unhesitatingly, I laid out three dollars, a not inconsiderable sum for me in 1947. It wasn't until some hours later that I found the author's autograph on the title page. It was Ray Bradbury's first book, and now worth, according to some lists, as much as $225 when in mint condition with its dust jacket. It should be noted, however, lest the finances of book collecting be taken too seriously, that certain stocks bought forty years ago, and any number of commodities, would be worth a great deal more in terms of percentage increase. Still, if I cared to sell, I could make a tidy profit! But I have no such intention, barring some life-saving need, like an emergency appendix transplant.

One of my more unusual rarities evokes a name once very common in French classes, but now, I suspect, almost unknown to most students: Tartarin. This brilliant creation of Alphonse Daudet was a Frenchman from the little southern town of Tarascon, where the natives, sun-struck in a way, seem to dwell in a world of exaggeration, daydreams and highly colored fantasies. Tartarin is their leader, and the greatest dreamer of all. In a superb feat of characterization, Daudet shows how Tartarin is perpetually at war with himself, one personality being that of the reckless, valiant, idealistic Don Quixote, the other the quibbling, fireplace-hugging, practical Sancho Panza. A most delectable book, Daudet's *Tartarin de Tarascon*. There was an equally delightful sequel, *Tartarin sur les Alps*, too, but the rarity I refer to is the third, and last, of the series, *Port-Tarascon*. It has much of the same ebullience and humor, but also a somber side, as the inhabitants of Tarascon, led by Tartarin, fall for a nasty scam involving a colony on a far-off island in Polynesia. The advertisement read:

FREE COLONY OF PORT-TARASCON.
For sale, lands at five francs the acre,
bringing in several millions of francs a year.
Fortune rapid and assured.
Colonists wanted.

The Don Quixote in Tartarin sounds the appeal, "Cover yourself with glory!" but the Sancho Panza alter ego murmurs doubtfully, "Cover yourself with flannel!"

The intriguing aspect of this book, however, is the nature of its numerous illustrations; they are the first, according to a history of photography, to be made from actual photos, instead of being, as had always been the case before, woodcuts, engravings, etchings and the like.

This lovely, sturdy, magnificently bound and elegantly printed book, published in 1891, was, I might add, discarded by a library some years ago, and became all mine for twenty-five cents.

Over some sixty years I've acquired, for modest sums, quite a number of rare books, and still prowl the thrift shops of the Bay Area in search of others. Not long ago, in the SPCA shop, I found the splendid ten-volume set, all thick, heavy, sturdy folios, that comprise *The Century Dictionary and Cyclopedia*, a famous publication that rivals the *Oxford English Dictionary* in its many historical citations on word usage. It first appeared in the 1889 to 1891 period; two of the volumes deal with proper names and geography only. A wonderful reference, still very useful after ninety years.

As a sometime writer of science fiction and fantasy, it's natural that many of my rarities are books in those fields. I have, for example, *Skull-Face and Others*, by Robert E. Howard, the creator of Conan. This 1946 short-story collection, in a rather worn dust jacket, cost me five dollars new, and now sells for sixty dollars or more.

A science fiction work with far more literary value is my first edition of Rudyard Kipling's *With the Night Mail: A Story of 2000 A.D.* This tale originally appeared in the November 1905 issue of *McClure's Magazine*. The copy I have is the 1909 Doubleday edition (its first appearance in book form), a slim, elegant little volume with a nicely decorated cover. The story deals with Kipling's idea of airborne mail delivery by means of "Postal Packets," which are ship-like, propeller-driven craft. Alas, like so many prophets in the field of technology, Kipling is far off the mark; his invention suggests the Victorian gussied up in the manner of the charming TV show, *The Wild Wild West*. But, as always, the writing is superb, so the story is well worth reading. And there are a few hints here and there of prophecy that is valid.

Not all rare books are valuable. I have before me now one that surely would be very hard to find. It is *The Refugee*, by Herman Melville. This novel, a rather satirical and amusing one about the early days of our Revolutionary War, with a cynical put-down of some Founding Fathers, was originally called *Israel Potter*. My version, bound in red, was published in 1865 as part of Peterson's reprint series, ten years after the first edition. As I say, not found in any old bookstore, but worth—who knows? Not a great deal, I suspect. But I'm very glad to have it; 1865, after all, was a year when Melville still walked this Earth. This copy, found in a junk store about 1949, cost me all of fifteen cents.

Getting back to Howard, I have all the Gnome Press first edition Conan books in dust jackets, well preserved, and the complete Skylark novels of another famous writer in the genre, Edward E. Smith. These are bringing high prices today, but are hardly of literary value compared to Melville!

I could go on with others. My collection includes *Battles and Leaders of the Civil War*, in four massive volumes, original editions, but, unfortunately, missing a total of about five pages that were torn out for the illustrations. Still, a bargain at a buck each! And my late nineteenth-century volume of the famous mathematics texts of Isaac Todhunter, crammed with those incredibly difficult and complicated problems used on the famous Tripos examinations, sailed through by such greats as James Clerk Maxwell, William Thomson (Lord Kelvin) and Sir George Stokes. A mere glimpse of these today would send most graduate math students into shock!

On the other hand, there are all the chances I missed. When I was a boy, early novels by Hemingway, Fitzgerald and Faulkner could be found for the price of a good restaurant dinner, but I didn't even look, having no great fondness for the writers then. And, I must admit, not much more now, believing Dickens and Hardy a lot better. So no regrets—I bought what I enjoyed reading, not for monetary gain, although it doesn't depress me to think about current prices for about twenty-five out of several thousand books I've owned.

And, finally, it's still a low-grade fever in the blood; I can't pop into any used-book shop or thrift store, no matter how well ransacked before, day after day, without anticipatory stirrings of my spirit. It's not so much the actual finding, perhaps, as the hunt.

Moments of Poignancy

It has been wisely noted that war consists of long periods of boredom punctuated by moments of sheer terror. The same could be said for many dangerous occupations like police work and fire-fighting. Somewhat similarly, most of us would agree that our lives, if carefully and objectively evaluated, would show days, months, even years, during which we marked time, so to speak, punctuated by memorable, flashlit intervals of joy, pain, delight and despair, all of varying degree and duration.

There is, however, another class of remembered events, usually small, fleeting, outwardly almost trivial, involving our own personal feelings, certainly not of national concern, but still hauntingly resonant, which remain tenaciously on some floppy disc of the brain. They could be called moments of poignancy.

The earliest such experience I can recall occurred when I was about seven years old. My mother, as I learned later, since she died when I was nine, liked cats, and always managed to have one about the house or yard. The earlier ones I have no memory of, being too young and involved with the "buzzing, blooming confusion" of infancy, but one sad vision persists. Our cat—actually a kitten, I think—was dying. It crouched on the shabby, grey-hued porch with its mouth open, struggling to breathe. Now, at that time, about 1921, few people thought of taking any pet to a vet, just as they never dreamed of packaged or canned food for them. The animals lived mainly on table-scraps and what they could scrounge from the noisome garbage cans in littered alleys. So our little cat, poisoned by something or other, sat forlornly on the stoop choking to death. My mother, I'm sure, was unhappy about it, but death came easily even to people then, as it did to her only three years later, so the death of a hapless kitten was only a minor tragedy. Can one still mourn for a mongrel kitten dead almost seventy years? I don't go that far, but the poignant moment is seared into my memory for good.

The next poignancy occurred much later, on one of those dirty, draughty, crowded Chicago streetcars on which I was riding to high school one morning. It was a long trip, since we had moved quite a distance recently, yet I wanted to stay with my classmates, and so opted for a tiresome daily commute rather than a transfer. I had just settled into a seat, and lucky to find one, when I became aware of two people across from me. Both were female and black, although in those days the terms Negro or "colored" would have been used by polite whites, and very nasty names tossed off, often less from malice or rudeness than sheer, unconscious racism. One was nothing unusual, just a large, motherly looking woman of about forty, with sad eyes and a melancholy air about her. The other, presumably her daughter, looked about fifteen, and was truly exceptional. She was badly deformed, with a hunched back not helped by shabby, ill-fitting—what could fit?—clothing. That was not an edifying sight, but when she spoke, I began to wince physically and psychologically, for she had a monstrous speech defect, caused, perhaps, as I've thought in retrospect, by a cleft palate or the like. And as if that were not enough, I gradually realized the poor girl was also blind. My whole being shuddered with that terrible revelation. I was a thoughtless kid, more interested in the Cubs (the Chicago baseball team), my dates, few and unsatisfactory, and the boring regimen of school, than the irremediable injustices of the world, but that encounter was a true moment of poignancy I've never forgotten. I know nothing about the deformed girl or her ultimate fate, nor do I know, not having been able to understand her speech, whether she was also—mercifully, perhaps—mentally retarded, unaware of what her life held in store for her. But she will stay, forever fifteen and tragic, in my memory, as will her brooding mother, charged with her care in a callous, often racist, world.

Those first two moments of poignancy were clearly dark, unrelieved by any kind of humor; but the next, although still rather sad, was, to some extent, a sort of tragicomic story.

In 1946, housing in Los Angeles was still very tight: that was the bad news, an apartment vacancy rate close to zero. The good news was that some rent-control legislation applied, so as a college math instructor, I was able to get a small apartment with a fold-down bed and other furnishings for thirty dollars a month—after I gave the manager a "gift" of fifty, something pretty well taken for granted in the housing market.

The building was big, and rather run-down, consisting of three floors, each with six apartments. In such a place, at that time, there was no shortage of poignant ironies of coexistence among varied transients who lived there. On the third floor, for example, in a corner room, was a young woman, far from attractive, who, perhaps because she was dazzled by attentions rarely offered her in peacetime, had become pregnant by a soldier who promptly vanished on learning about her condition. She was the only mother in the building, with an infant to raise, and the Pecksniffs didn't make it easy. They complained about the smells, the crying, and the whole idea of so immoral a creature in their midst. To be fair, some were tolerant and helpful; but the young woman, to my gaze, always seemed dejected, even distraught. Well, that was probably a far from uncommon little tragedy in wartime; the poignancy I remember more vividly was unique.

Living on the same floor with me was an elderly woman, quite reclusive, since I rarely saw her at all. I had only fleeting glimpses of her as she furtively came and went, invariably—no matter the weather, often very warm in a Los Angeles summer—wearing a long, black, highly unstylish overcoat, one that didn't even seem designed for women, but men—or Martians. That was one of two oddities about her; the other was the puzzling smell, vaguely hot, moist and soapy that seeped from her room every night about the same time, around seven. The solution to this mystery came to me from the manager herself, a petty thief and sneaky spy on the tenants—she would go into their apartments when they were out to snoop and, if the risk was small, steal something she could sell in order to buy liquor, for she was an alcoholic. She told me one day, when I raised the question, that the tenant, who worked for the city in some minor position, had an irrational fear of germs and infections, and so, every night, she boiled the overcoat! This, in fact, took up so much of her evenings that she had almost no social life. I was appalled and saddened; what a waste of a human being and potential, however limited basically. A poignant moment that also sticks. I still don't know how she was able to carry out this operation on a tiny gas stove, but suppose she had a giant metal pot of the sort used by our grandmothers to do laundry in, and took whatever time was needed to bring gallons of water to a boil each night. No wonder a washday smell!

Now here are two vignettes, related, if tenuously, from the Great Depression. In 1933, my older brother, who had been laid off from a job at the phone company, obtained for him there by my father, who was a Bell Telephone pioneer with a lifetime job guarantee because of a train accident that had taken his right arm, did what others in that fix had done, and tried going into business on his own. It was hopeless, of course, even with a really good product and expert salesmanship, but he opted for selling neckties by mail, and in a one-man office downtown limped along for a few months rarely making even his tiny expenses.

As a teen, I was helping him out. There were no wages, but I did get breakfast—seventeen cents then, I swear, for an egg, toast and coffee—and lunch, both eaten at a cheap, popular downtown restaurant.

One of the few customers who somehow came in from the street was what we'd call today a bag lady. Of indeterminate age, she was shapeless, weirdly dressed in assorted rags, and definitely under par mentally. With all the insensitivity of my age and temperament, I nicknamed her—not to her face; I had at least that much civility— Kid Frowse, an invention that vastly amused my older brother, although he was generally far more compassionate than I. It should have been a trivial encounter, but somehow, if not at first, the sad predicament of the old woman, and my inexcusable attitude, came back to me years later, and stuck painfully, as a poignant moment. Incidentally, we never knew how or where she sold the few neckties she bought from us with some grubby coins, slowly and tortuously extracted from a dark recess of her clothing.

The related vignette concerns my father. He came downtown daily on the "L", and each morning bought a newspaper, then about three cents. He would read it during the trip, and was amazingly deft in folding it neatly with one hand so as to peruse each page in turn, an action that bemused his fellow riders—and me, if I happened to be with him, occasionally the case.

Then, as he came to the stairs of the "L" for the return trip, he would hand the paper to whoever was first in line among the jobless, often homeless, men and women who waited for them, either to search for non-existent jobs or as a padding against the brutal winds that blew off Lake Michigan.

And once, when I had left my brother's office in time to join my father for the ride home, I saw him quickly, furtively make some odd movement into the pages of the paper, neatly folded, as usual. When I asked him about it, he told me, very diffidently, perhaps because he was naturally shy about his softer impulses, or thought his sons, in view of our very restricted income—he was taking one unpaid day off a week, so other company men could also work—might object, that he sometimes put a dollar bill between the pages. That was a poignant moment I didn't fully appreciate then, but one which has touched me often since.

The next event was actually much more than a poignant moment; it was, in fact, the major tragedy of my life, but couldn't possibly seem so when it occurred, because I was simply too young, at nine, to understand the deeper implications.

My mother, after an apparently healthy girlhood, had somehow, while still a young woman, developed a serious chronic illness. Medical science at that time didn't give us a clear explanation of its nature, but, looking back, I suspect it was a kind of congestive heart failure, characterized by fluid in the lungs, and great, even life-threatening, difficulty in breathing. On the terrible night in question, she had suddenly suffered a very bad attack, and was propped up in bed, gasping for breath. Since our regular doctor, for some reason, was not available, my father, in desperation, called in a neighborhood GP, who knew nothing about her particular case. No doubt he did his best, but, in hindsight, and from what can be inferred, must have been grossly incompetent, for he gave her something not merely useless, but strongly counter-indicated for her condition: morphine. And so, quietly, peacefully, and wholly unnecessarily, she died. It seems now like a macabre mockery of the kitten's death

My father was a tough, resilient little man, who, as an immigrant speaking almost no English, had made his way among a welter of other new Americans—Poles, Italians, Greeks, Russians and Germans—in Chicago, becoming, of necessity, quite handy with his fists. Before long, after holding many jobs, he became fluent and accentless in colloquial English, and was a literate, competent employee of the Bell Telephone Company, specializing in right-of-way.

I had never seen him show a lot of emotion, although he was clearly fond of, and kind to, his family; so you can imagine the effect on me, a child, to hear coming from the bedroom a dreadful, animal-like keening as he repeatedly called his wife's name, begging her not to die, to "come back" to him. He must have loved her greatly, far more than we, his four sons, realized then, for although he lived into his eighties, he never remarried, and apparently had not even one romantic attachment to any other woman. Long after, studying Shakespeare in high school, the immensely moving scene in which King Lear cradles the dead Cordelia in his arms, wailing, "Thou'lt come no more, Never, never, never, never, never!" seemed a commentary on that night of despair. Yet it was, in effect, only a poignant moment, an explosive disruption of my stream of consciousness, which had not been flowing long; because I have never been able to recall any other details of my mother's death. Perhaps I blocked it out for good as a thought that lies too deep for tears.

It may seem a little bizarre to feel, or pretend to, another person's poignant moment; yet I read about a grim event some years ago that has haunted me ever since, almost as if I'd been there to witness it. But the victim was a total stranger whom I'd never met, seen at a distance, or even heard of before.

The odd situation, as reported in various news media, was basically a simple and familiar one; a car crash. A young man, while driving to his office, was involved in what seemed little more than a fender bender. He was not seriously injured in the sense of major trauma to his body, but, unfortunately, got a hard enough blow from something—the wheel, perhaps—to injure his throat, completely closing the airway. With ninety-nine percent of us, we would have died without a fighting chance, ignorant of what to do. But the true poignancy in this case, and why it so affected me, is that the victim was a brilliant young doctor with a very promising career ahead of him. Desperate to survive, and fully aware of what was needed to do so, he held off suffocation almost by sheer effort of will, pulled a small pen knife from his pocket, and attempted a hasty tracheotomy—the cutting of an opening directly through the skin and cartilage just above his Adam's apple, into the trachea, which would have allowed the free flow of air to his lungs.

It was a gallant, icy-nerved try, but luck was against him. Unable to complete the comparatively simple operation, one he no doubt found easy even as a green intern, he lost consciousness and died. Nobody was there to tell the story, which was inferred, I believe, when he was found slumped over the wheel, knife in hand, with significant cuts on his neck. Not my own tragedy, but the memory of it is a poignant moment to me.

And now to end on a lighter, but still poignant, note. I come to the most recent occurrence. A few years ago, when my morning walk took me near Fisherman's Wharf in Monterey, I was moving along with the rapid, loping gait that has always been my natural pace. (In his collections of essays, *The Autocrat of the Breakfast Table*, Oliver Wendell Holmes Sr. had speculated more than a century ago, perhaps rightly, that a person's legs are like pendulums in having a mathematically defined swing based on their length. Mine are long!) Suddenly, I became aware of company; a young boy, about ten years old, was trotting beside me. (His legs, predictably, were a lot shorter!) A little breathlessly, he said he'd seen me several times before, and felt admiration that an "old guy" like me could be thin, vigorous and capable of sustaining that kind of a stride. That was good to hear; who among us is completely free of vanity, or, for that matter, immune to flattery? But the poignancy came when he added that his own father, younger than I, was fat, soft, lethargic and, in general, pretty much a mess. "I wish he was like you," he concluded wistfully.

What could I say? Honor thy father? I'm the last one qualified to quote, much less thump, the Bible, or to play Bay Area hedge-parson, so I could only mumble that his father may have had other excellent qualities more important than leanness and a long-legged step. Nor would there have been any point in discussing with the child the terrible, cold, merciless judgments the young make of the old at times. I'm sure that what I did say was of little use, and can only hope that the years brought them closer together, that the father shaped up a bit, and the son became more tolerant. But the poignancy of that moment has lingered.

There are other poignant moments that are not my own, but which continue to move me when I think of them occasionally. To draw on John Donne's famous poem, we needn't assume the bells tolled just for some people far removed from us in space and time, but for all mankind as well.

As a young boy, years ago, I ran across, and was touched by, another poem, on Eleanor Freeman, who died in 1650, aged twenty-one. I still wonder what she was like compared to her peers today, and think about Poe's observation that there is a unique pathos in the early death of a lovely girl.

And I also recall a similar, even sadder occurrence recorded in the great diary of Samuel Pepys. In a casual, detached way, he notes that a young servant girl, who was a little deformed, had suddenly hanged herself for no apparent reason. No apparent reason! I think about her life of hard work and probably harder blows, the penalty for being born into the wrong class in seventeenth-century England, and how after perhaps twelve or fifteen hours of exhausting, dirty chores, she was given the boon of resting in a cold, drab, dark, tiny garret, where she could ponder two or three more decades of the same. And I grieve for her, just a little, now and then.

Although I'm far from religious, and reject the idea of an afterlife, I have to respond much as Mark Twain, equally skeptical, did, on reading this epitaph in a Baden-Baden cemetery, which he reported in *A Tramp Abroad*:

Here Reposes in God,
Caroline de Clery,
a Religieuse of St. Denis aged 83 years—and blind.
The light was restored to her in Baden the 5th of January, 1839.

Twain was greatly moved, as am I. A most poignant epitaph!

Memoirs of a
Harried Peninsula Hiker

After coming to the Monterey Bay Area, with its entrancing scenery and sea-scented air, such a change from the poisonous gases bathing Los Angeles, which the inhabitants now consider to be normal, I became a hardcore walker. I'd always enjoyed such activity, but now I began to get up very early, often before dawn, and cover twelve to fifteen miles, going at a rate of about five miles an hour. I would start from my home base near the Pacific Grove Post Office and explore. My favorite route was down Central into Monterey; from there, I might return via the ocean, continuing to the golf course or beyond; or go to Seaside. Occasionally, I went to Carmel, rather a wearing hike because of the steep climb up Holman Highway.

These trips were like a university without walls, what with the experiences and encounters—odd, amusing and sometimes quite scary.

There were, inevitably, serpents in the Eden, both two- and four-legged, against all the laws of biology. The first of these were drivers, who for some reason seem to hate pedestrians. They would yell obscenities and threats, although I was not in their way, being either on the sidewalk or the shoulder of the highway.

On the other hand, there were a few who were very friendly. One truck driver who regularly delivered in Monterey always honked at me and called out a friendly greeting. And often, when I got to busier areas as the sun moved higher, strangers would come up, and say they'd seen me all over the Bay Area and thought it was great the way I got around on foot. This was before the jogging craze, and I met very few people; sometimes none at all before reaching a business district. I was amazed that nobody seemed to appreciate the superb views.

The other serpents finally, in fact, drove me from much of Paradise, the side streets with their fascinating houses I so enjoyed seeing. I refer to dogs. Now admittedly, I'd always been a "cat man," but had no particular bias against dogs: "Live and let live" was my creed. But after being harassed for years while strolling along, minding my own business, I developed a profound dislike for the species. By the same token, I became a great admirer of the leopard, a gorgeous spotted cat, the favorite food of which, I learned, was—you guessed it—dog. A leopard, hunters say, will unhesitatingly pass up Pheasant Under Glass for Terrier Tartare. My kind of beast.

It's probably true that barking dogs rarely bite, but as an old joke goes: you know it and I know it, but does the dog know it?

Attempting to solve the problem, I adapted a little plastic squeeze-bottle as an ammonia sprayer. I hoped never to have to use it, doubting its efficacy against a large, ferocious animal. But I did get one chance to find out. Like so much in life, the test was ambiguous. When a huge collie ran out to snap at my heels, I thrust the bottle towards his face and squeezed. Alas, there was a strong breeze, which dissipated the stream, and the dog, while shaking its head in distaste, seemed more puzzled than intimidated. I loped out of his territory and escaped unharmed, if shaken. Needless to say, on these encounters no owner was ever around, a clear violation of the law.

The worst experience was quite unexpected. Up on High Street, after leaving the Presidio, a favorite goal, I chanced to pass a young girl leading a large, white dog. Assuming, foolishly, that this at least was a safe combination, I brushed by. To my shock, the brute buried its teeth in my thigh. Unless one has been bitten, they can have no idea of the immense power of a big dog's jaws.

I limped to the Monterey police station, displayed the bleeding wound and complained. I had a hard time, for some reason, getting officials—who had learned it from my information—to give me the dog owner's name, but finally succeeded. I then harried him into paying my medical bill, mainly for an anti-tetanus shot. But he had the gall, typical of many irresponsible people, to write on the check that this one fifteen-dollar payment released him from any other charges. What if the wound became infected? What if—unlikely, but such things happen—the animal's rabies shots failed? I crossed out his demurrer and, luckily, had no problems.

To backtrack briefly, soon after coming to Pacific Grove, I thought that a bicycle would be ideal for getting around, allowing me to cover much more ground than on foot, so I bought a fine multi-geared model. Although I'd not ridden one for decades, the knack quickly returned; as they say, one never really forgets a physical skill. I used it for only a few months, however, chiefly for trips to Seaside, where I hunted used books, splendid buys, at the Goodwill Industries Shop. But I learned fast that to most drivers bicycles were either invisible or much like cats to self-respecting dogs: something to be killed or, at least, driven up a tree. So after a number of bad scares on Del Monte, very busy in the morning, I wisely concluded that walking was not only a lot safer, but more relaxing and also better for sightseeing and window shopping.

Memory is a spotty, inexplicable thing. I once met a tall, strongly built old man who had been all over the world in the 1920s. We talked for about an hour while walking along beautiful Ocean View Boulevard to Lovers Point, yet the only part of that conversation that remains is his delightful story about a contrast between England and France. In England, he told me, there are chickens everywhere; anybody with even a tiny yard keeps them, but—and this was the paradox—it was almost impossible to buy a chicken dinner. Why were the fowls kept, and what became of them? Did the owners eat them all? And in France, one never saw a chicken at large, yet every restaurant had a dozen varieties on the menu; where did the birds come from? I wonder if the situation still obtains today; not being a world traveler, or one who cares to go any place not attainable on foot, I may never know.

Some macabre visions still linger, like my seeing, near the Pacific Grove crematorium, a van unloading a number of coffins, each a *memento mori* for a fine morning. And nearby, deer, graceful, tame—and greedy—eating the flowers left for the dead.

And the sight, much more pleasant, of gaudy magpies, which I'd never seen elsewhere, almost a match for the peacocks that used to live at the Naval Postgraduate School.

And something I saw far too often, that enraged me to the point of murder: people in cars throwing bags of garbage not only into our streets, but even into yards. I may have some lingering doubts about capital punishment, but none about applying it to these swine.

Some encounters were more pleasant, or at least intriguing. For example, I met almost daily a counterpart of sorts, a lone hiker, rather shaggy, always accompanied by—yes—a dog, but one that was fat and good-natured. We would exchange greetings, and on one occasion he told me he was too radical for this society and had become a kind of outcast. And later, when he came by dogless and glum, he told me his enemies had stolen his pet, just to hurt him.

Before long, however, he found a replacement, also a peaceful animal.

Almost as bad as the mean dogs, by the way, were the over-friendly ones that annoyed me greatly. Bored and lonely, with owners, I presume, who did not walk, they would latch on to me as if I'd invited them, accompanying me, literally, for miles, ignoring my shouts, gestures and threats. Several times I was reduced to holing up in a phone booth until the pest gave up on me and followed somebody else. With other walkers so scarce, that didn't always work.

Another hiker I met almost daily was a small person with a nut-brown face. It—I use the pronoun intentionally—was always muffled in garments that made it shapeless, so it was only after about a year that what I took for a little man proved to be a little woman.

Another recurring pattern was fun; I mean the finding of so many things, mostly coins. These would turn up singly or in strange batches. I guessed that groups of coins near the curb must have spilled out of drivers' pockets as they scrambled or writhed into badly designed cars. In any case, I found enough loose change to pay all my postage. And once I picked up a sizeable amount of paper money. Although I advertised, nobody ever claimed it—a puzzler—so I was about fifty dollars richer.

There were many things I didn't bother to pick up—a million combs, for example. And there were foolers: bottle-caps, when the sun glints on them, look very much like coins, so I'd stoop, reach, then sigh or swear, my hope of a quarter dashed.

Loping down streets very early, I often saw our nocturnal fauna coming home from the night's operations: raccoons, opossums, once a rabbit (somebody's pet, I'm sure), and one really amazing sight: a lithe, looping, graceful little weasel.

One of my favorite hikes was to the Naval Postgraduate School with its verdant grounds and lovely little lagoon. I wanted to visit the off-limits areas, so sent a letter, pointing out I didn't smoke or litter and wanted only to walk about and enjoy. Much to my surprise, a few days later there was a knock on my door and who should it be but the commandant himself, a man of Finnish origin and a true gentleman, who told me he was himself a dedicated hiker and approved my request, giving me a fine letter to carry. And it came in handy, because the first time I entered verboten territory a huge MP, able and no doubt willing to pinch off my head with two fingers, became quite friendly when I produced the letter.

A basic problem of these long walks was the matter of heels. At, say, twelve miles a day, I was doing almost four hundred a month, something no rubber or composite, however tough, can take, and the days of the buck replacement are long gone. So what to do if insolvency was to be avoided? I found an excellent solution. I bought a package of one hundred one-inch wood screws, which I drove into the heels, mainly along the edges, hobnail fashion. (Hobnails, themselves, it seems, once common in laborer's boots, are also gone.) So armored, a heel lasts a year; even longer, if additional screws are strategically added as the shoe wears. Soles, for some reason, last much longer on their own.

Like some drivers, the police also may harass early-morning walkers. I was stopped several times, but was always treated courteously, if with some coldness. Usually when I'd say, half-facetiously, that I was a poor prospect for criminal activity, being a retired Army officer, ex-college professor, born wimp and fairly long of tooth, the cop would agree I was harmless and turn me loose.

As all know, however, cops will seek us out handily, but if you need one ...! Very early one chilly autumn morning, I was passing the Presidio entrance at Bolio Road near the tunnel, when I was hailed by a plaintive voice from the shrubbery. It belonged to a hapless fellow who had been robbed, he said, and stripped of his clothes. Shivering and miserable, I assumed, he was delighted to see, at last, somebody come by. I promised him I'd hurry on and call the police from the first phone booth, and did my best; but there were no booths around. I hoped to spot and flag down a cruiser, but no luck in that either. Finally, about twenty minutes later, with most businesses not yet open, I went into a hotel, just coming to life, mainly in the dining room, and persuaded them to make the call.

But what finally happened, whether the man's story was true, or whether it was a more arcane matter—some kind of tryst that went wrong, for example, as the cynical skeptic in me wondered—I never did learn, alas; but, like the legendary piano player in the house of ill-fame, I did my damnedest.

Something should be said about one constant dilemma typical of this area—what on Earth should one wear when starting out for a three-hour hike in the morning? Often, when no rain was predicted, or at least not before late afternoon, I'd leave under a totally clear, starry sky (by the way, checking out Orion and the other "easy" constellations and planets, was one of the additional joys of my jaunts) only to find, when five hopeless miles from home, that clouds can roll in from somewhere in a matter of minutes, followed by nasty downpours.

Getting back then, was a problem, but I had one fairly good technique, which was to aim for the clearest part of the sky, even if that meant a roundabout return. Often it worked, and I would arrive home only slightly damp. Sometimes it was a complete failure and I'd reach my house looking like a pile of wet laundry. But I never caught a cold and, in fact, haven't had one in the last thirty years. What that proves, I know not, except that, as doctors say, mere wind and rain are not important factors in such illnesses. But weather has no brother, so to speak, and nobody can fight that big City Hall in the Sky; if you care to live here, you accept the climate—and gratefully.

A few sidelights from my walker's diary:

I was never mugged or seriously menaced by people—only by dogs. That was due in part to my following the recommended defensive techniques. I walked always with brisk purposefulness, never looking or acting like a potential victim, although any vigorous young male could have easily decked me, a skinny 130 pounds of aging wimp. Once, in Seaside, a husky black man, on passing me, roared out a mischievous, "Boo!" hoping to startle an intruding honky, but I didn't jump, kept a wooden face and moved on. To be sure, I had my squeeze-bottle ready to give him a faceful of ammonia should he actually attack, but nothing like that happened.

I also avoided any groups that looked or sounded rowdy, by detouring, if necessary, and scuttling down a different street before they saw me.

Well, that was years ago, but I still see my friendly truck driver occasionally, in or around Pacific Grove. He hails me and wonders why we haven't met in Monterey and Seaside, so I explain.

As for the little, heavily-muffled hiker with the brown, wrinkly face, she told me several years ago that she had to move to a large city on the East Coast—a terrible fate, I thought: heat, humidity and horrendous expenses for housing and other amenities. But she didn't seem to mind and gave me her address, asking me to write. I'm not much for casual correspondence, but hate to offend anybody of good will, so we did exchange a few letters. I found her, as expected, literate and bright but a little too pious for my taste, and the writing faded away.

And my fellow loner, still looking like a 1960s overage hippie, with his dog, now grossly fat—since together they walk many miles each day, as before, it must be a matter, not of too little exercise, but a gluttonous diet, and since its master is thin, the animal is the better fed of the two—gets to Pacific Grove now and then. And urban survivalist that he is, cadges a free breakfast at World Savings, insolently striding in to have a coffee and cookies as if a bona fide customer—which ain't bloody likely.

Not all my peculiar little encounters were restricted to the road. Now that I'm more of a homebody, events and portents zero in at my house. A few weeks ago, for example, I was just awakening from an afternoon nap when I heard a sweet, ladylike voice on the walk outside. "Come on, Baby," it said. "You can do it! Come, Darling." I quickly inferred the woman's cat had gone up something—a tree, probably—and she was trying to coax it down. "Come, Baby," she cooed again. Then, when there was no result, the voice hardened, became strident and she roared, "Oh $&#%!" using a four-letter word once reserved for uninhibited men. Whether it shocked the cat into descending, I don't know, but from then on there was silence, and I chuckled.

Not so funny was an occurrence a bit later, at three a.m., in fact, early one morning. There was a rather diffident knock at my bedroom door, which opens onto the street, the house being on a corner lot with two such entrances, this the side one, actually.

"Who's there?" I asked, and the intruder gave his name, which I'll not reveal.

"What do you want?" I demanded querulously.

In an aggrieved voice he said, "I want to come in; I live here."

"You're drunk or crazy," I blurted out. "This is a private residence."

"No," he insisted. "It's my townhouse; I recognize the front door." Then he added quietly and, I admit, convincingly: "I don't drink. I'm on the Board of Something-or-Other," he continued, to prove his status as a sober public official.

Now any resemblance between my run-down, shabby building with its weedy yard and a townhouse is totally unbelievable, and I said so. After we argued for a few minutes, he even told me his wife was inside and he had to join her. Exasperated, I got out of bed, opened the door and said bitterly: "Look, for God's sake—it's a bedroom. How could this be your townhouse?" But not even that display convinced him and finally I asked: "What street is your house on?"

"Lighthouse."

"Hell!" I said. "This is Laurel. Lighthouse is that way," and I gestured.

There was a brief, pregnant silence. Then my strange visitor said very politely, in measured tones, "Thank you," and left.

"You're welcome," I replied, with heavy irony, having lost an hour's sleep by this insanity. But the real point is a mysterious one: what would make a sober man, a solid citizen, mistake a small, decrepit house for an apartment in a presumably well maintained townhouse? To add to the confusion, my caller, whose shadowy figure seemed to me rather small, his manner meek, held a package of what looked like bakery goods. Was he bringing his wife some pastry to divert her wrath at his late return? Alas, I shall never know!

Well, in days long past, before age, angina and laziness grounded me so that I'm lucky to rack up four miles a day in two stints, I was known to the late Dick Bragg—he of the rich, deep, warm voice and unflappable good nature whose local radio talk show I called often—as "The Walker."

There are worse names.

Still Writing and Selling at Eighty-Four

Yesterday, exactly a week after I turned eighty-four, I revised and mailed a short story to a national magazine that has just printed an earlier one of mine. I won't name it, but it's one of the few left—there were many in the 1950s—still hospitable to my kind of writing, which is definitely not "serious" in the Hemingway tradition, but more a matter of clever plot gimmicks than character. It pays, I add gratefully, a generous twenty-five cents a word, more than some better known, prestigious publications.

Yes, I'm boasting, both for my own satisfaction, egotistical, admittedly, and to make the important point that age does not always trump creativity. But mainly I'm pumped up because I truly doubt there are many octogenarians out there still writing and selling fiction.

Since my first success, way back in 1950, when I sent a short fantasy titled "Modeled in Clay" to a fly-by-night magazine, long gone, named *Man to Man*, and gazed with extreme delight at a fifty-dollar check some weeks later, I've sold well over 300 more, counting numerous reprints. One science fiction tale, "The Ruum," has resurfaced over twenty-five times—here and abroad, in various languages and anthologies.

I've never made a living from writing; very few do, earning in my best year about $6,000; and the most I ever got for a short story was $1,000 from *Cosmopolitan*. I got the money, yes, but the story was never printed, a bit of very bad luck for me, because exactly at that time the magazine was turned over to Helen Gurley Brown, and my mystery, although quite good and offbeat, was not suitable for her needs, alas. It broke my heart, but the story was indeed good, and resold immediately to a men's magazine for $400, a good consolation prize. But I desperately wanted a breakthrough to the big time, the "slicks," as they were called, and felt very bitter.

However, I didn't need or expect to live on my earnings from writing, since my real, paying profession was that of a college math teacher, and I could regard the scribbling as a hobby. And, of course, it was great fun, with bursts of real delight when something sold or a story made some "best of" anthology, as did the *Cosmopolitan* one, "The Reason."

My creativity was not limited to fiction, although most of my sales were in the fields of detective and science fiction. I also sold at least fifty essays and poems—of the latter, only about six of those were passably good; my light verse was, I think, better—but only locally. I still long to have a poem in some national magazine, but writing a decent poem is the toughest chore there is; the competition is brutal, the markets very small, the number of aspiring poets depressingly large and prolific, so I honestly rate my chance as small and none! But I don't plan to quit any time soon.

And there are a few totally different achievements I can look back on with much pleasure. I've made, and published in suitable professional journals, several minor but gratifying discoveries in mathematics; and even got a mention for a new math-based cipher-method in *The Codebreakers*, David Kahn's Bible on the history and techniques of cryptography.

I should add, as an amusing sidebar, that one of my stories combined fiction with mathematics, with interesting consequences. It was "The Devil and Simon Flagg," about a math teacher who wins a highly dangerous bet with Satan by challenging him to prove—or disprove—the famous conjecture of the great mathematician, Pierre de Fermat. This extremely difficult problem, which baffled the finest researchers for centuries, was just recently solved by Andrew Wiles. Well, my decades-old tale was reprinted in a new account of the theorem, and Marilyn vos Savant also mentioned it in her shorter, less technical book on the subject.

Perhaps I should add, with a nod to Frank Sinatra, that for the first forty-eight years I did it my way, on a series of three nearly indestructible Royal Standard manual typewriters. This year I got my first electric. Maybe at ninety-five, I'll try a word processor!

Finally, although some composers like Verdi and Saint-Saëns lived very long and produced great music, I rather doubt, as I mentioned before, there are many octogenarian writers still selling stories. I'll never make the big time now, but hope to keep publishing more potboiler, gimmicky short fiction, especially "locked room" mysteries, one of my specialties.

I took only one creative writing course; that was in college, sixty years ago, but learned a great deal just from reading such prosemeisters as Robert Louis Stevenson and Rudyard Kipling. As a child, though, I first read everything in a kind of frenzy of exploration, from Henrik Ibsen's *Peer Gynt*, which I only half comprehended, to Rafael Sabatini's bestsellers and a remarkably well crafted series of historical adventure books by Joseph Altsheler. Then there was a whole set of beautifully bound books, the complete essays of the brilliant French entomologist, Jean-Henri Fabre, whose accounts of insects in the field, even in translation, were marvels of exposition written in clear, elegant paragraphs. I played the "sedulous ape" to every writer I admired, never even knowing for sure why I thought them worth emulating. I'm convinced that for most would-be authors that's the best way—read, read, read in all fields, then write, revise carefully, and never stop, no matter what the calendar tells you!

Some of My Loose Ends and Minor Mysteries

In almost every person's life, I submit, there are a number of loose ends, gaps, anomalies, and small, unresolved mysteries that may tantalize us long after their occurrences. Did that particular event develop just as I recall it? Did it, in fact, happen at all, or am I fantasizing, distorting, or embellishing the experience of fifty years ago?

Who and what, for example, was the lovely young WAVE—Women Accepted for Volunteer Emergency Service, an auxiliary group associated with the Navy—that I dated so briefly and bittersweetly on the mighty streamliner train—surely it was the flashy, elegant *Super Chief*—from Chicago to Los Angeles in 1943? She was so cool and poised in her crisp, white uniform, much more so than the Army's WAACs—Women's Army Auxiliary Corps—in their drab khaki outfits. She was many cuts above my social class, but reluctantly, perhaps out of compassion or some sense of noblesse oblige, let me buy her lunch in the dining car with its glittering silver, white napkins, and suavely expert waiters, all new to me as a second lieutenant, gauche and a bit callow. Where is she now? Where are the snows of yesteryear?

And what of First Lieutenant Brownell, a recent Officer Candidate School graduate like the rest of us at Fort Sill,

Oklahoma—was he really assigned by Army Intelligence to spy on us, looking for subversives or even potential saboteurs? Barring a late miracle, I'll never know for sure about that or what became of my charming, patrician WAVE.

An early mystery in my life turned up about 1930, when, as a boy of fifteen, I was fascinated by science, and read avidly on the subject. Much of it was comprehended only vaguely, since I had no math beyond simple arithmetic, but I loved and respected the giants in the field—Newton, Maxwell, Darwin, Gauss and Einstein among many.

No such a titan, apparently, was one Alexander Gurvitch (1874-1954), who rattled some scientific cages at the time. He was a Russian biologist and pathologist who claimed to have discovered a new ray to go along with the not-so-old x-rays and cosmic rays. "Mitogenetic radiation"—that is to say, causing cell division—he called them, and said they were strong in sprouting plants, especially onions. What they could do, he declared, was spur growth in other, nearby vegetation.

I was much intrigued by this finding; not so the biological establishment, which ridiculed the claim, and soon it was excised from scientific literature, although the rays are still to be found in reference books now on library shelves.

Did such rays—do they?—exist? It would seem not, since they are not mentioned in modern books, and yet I infer from very recent experiments that plants indeed influence each other, that they flourish best when not alone, but in groups, perhaps by sending chemical messengers through the soil or air. Whether anybody has lately tried, with modern, sensitive equipment, to detect Gurvitch's mitogenetic rays, I don't know, but you see what I mean about small mysteries.

Scientists are sometimes faulted, with reason, for being too closed-minded, and it has happened, but a degree of conservatism is vital to the health of a discipline lest quackery flourish and false claims weaken the structure of science. Whatever is asserted must be rigorously proved a fact or, at least, a highly probable inference worth further testing.

I am not a professional researcher, so didn't go back in crumbling, yellow newspapers—or microfilms of them—from the 1930s, but have been unable to find Gurvitch's name in various biographical reference books more than twice.

A few years later, about 1940, came the Puzzle of the Pollen. At that time, and maybe even now, Chicago seemed like the ragweed capitol of the country; the hay fever in August was something fearsome to many of us. One day, a curious, cryptic article appeared in *The Chicago Tribune*. Somebody had been found, the report said, actually blowing ragweed pollen into the air with a giant fan mounted on a truck some miles from the city. What in the world was going on? Was it a medical experiment, benign in intent, to better understand how pollen spread? Or was some maker of antihistamines trying to improve business? As if we sneezers didn't already buy every remedy on the market! Chicago needed more ragweed pollen about as much as higher summer humidity.

Well, that story vanished after one day, and I never found out any more about the event. Yes, I'd still like to know!

In college, where I was thought to be a passable writer, the theatre group asked me to write a short play for them. New to that genre, I proceeded to comb the small library for collections of plays and hints about constructing "well made" ones.

In one obscure text, the title of which I no longer recall, there was a most remarkable one-act play—unique, probably—that impressed me greatly; so much, in fact, that years later I was still looking for a copy—in vain. The whole play consisted of only two words, which were repeated in a variety of circumstances; a bewitching, brilliant idea, a tour-de-force of ingenuity. The words were, "Come here," and before each use was the basic situation the actor had to master entirely by the inflection of his or her voice. For example:

Stern parent to child.
Lover to beloved.
Pompous boss to employee.
Impatient customer to waiter.
Woman sharing juicy gossip with friend.

There must have been, I think, a great many such tiny scenarios in the play. Despite scrutinizing yearbooks of the theatre for decades, I have never been able to find out who wrote the play, where it first was given, if it ever was, or where.

Not all my little mysteries are old, dusty and forgotten. Right now, here in beautiful, Practically Perfect Pacific Grove, there is one that has bemused me since my arrival in 1968. Almost every day during that period I've seen a woman who looks as if she'd be more typical of a neighborhood in Bulgaria or Albania. She wears, and has worn, I swear, for the whole two decades, the same peasant-like outfit consisting of a drab, shapeless dress, sometimes a ratty blue cloak, and always a headscarf or babushka. Not once has her apparel varied an iota. Even moi, as Miss Piggy—a very appropriate choice in my case!—would put it, clad in ill-fitting, thrift shop markdowns, whose interest in clothing would have to triple to approximate apathy, change my garments occasionally. But not the strange lady, who also tends to make sotto voce remarks to people she passes, who are not listening, and even to the air. Who is she, from where, and how is it she looked middle-aged in 1968, and still does?

Finally, we all know about those puzzling catchphrases, the obscure origins of which are constantly debated, like "Okay," "The whole nine yards," and "Twenty-three skidoo." My own favorite, which after my search of every reference book on quotations still eludes me, is "Good in spots, like the curate's egg." Its meaning is clear; it's an effective locution, but what novel, play, memoir, or whatever it comes from, I've not so far been able to find out. It has a less useful companion, equally mysterious: "Like taking the curl out of a pig's tail." In short, not possible—like finding solutions to all my nagging enigmas.

More Close Encounters
With the Fool-Killer

Sherlock Holmes, as most readers of the Canonical Works—the collected stories about the Baker Street immortal—will agree, did not suffer fools gladly. He was often all over the hapless Inspector Lestrade like a cheap suit; thought Edgar Allan Poe's cerebral C. Auguste Dupin something of a mountebank, and Gaboriau's plodding detective, LeCoq, a dimwit who took forever to resolve cases the Englishman would have cleared up in a day or two. He was even a bit impatient at times with the faithful, slightly obtuse Watson.

It has occurred to me that Sherlock Holmes may have shared genes, collaterally, with the Fool-Killer, since the latter, according to O. Henry, bore the name Jesse Holmes, at least in the South of this country.

As O. Henry describes him, the supernatural entity did not resemble Sherlock, but that is reasonable, since the relationship, if indeed it existed, was probably a distant one:

I remember the clear picture of him that hung on the walls of my fancy during my barefoot days when I was dodging his oft-threatened devoirs. To me, he was a terrible old man, in grey clothes, with a long, ragged, grey beard, and reddish, fierce eyes. I looked to see him come stumping up the road in a cloud of dust, with a white oak staff in his hand and his shoes tied with leather thongs. I may yet—

As a boy, I had no such picture of the Fool-Killer, and was totally unaware of his existence and *raison d'être*. But, looking back now, I realize all too well how often I merited his lethal attention.

In a previous essay, I cited some examples, and now add a few more, beginning with perhaps the worst and most painful, which put my younger brother at serious risk for his life.

I was fourteen, and he eleven. Our mother was dead, and our father, who never remarried, or—it goes without saying in those more conventional times—brought a woman to share our apartment, was doing his best to rear four sons, a tricky chore for a man on his own.

The miserable affair began as a simple pattern of truancy. We detested school, which was unpleasant at best. There was a lot of racial and ethnic tension; bullying went on frequently, unchecked by the teachers. My brother and I, to be honest, were a bit smug, being good students with a thirst for and appreciation of knowledge, and we both read very well. This degree of nerditude annoyed our peers, and we suffered for it.

Since my father and two older brothers left the house early, it was easy for us, when we should have started for school, just to remain at home. Once, when a brother came back soon after leaving, because he forgot something, we just slipped behind the upright piano until he departed again.

Our deception was made even easier by an odd circumstance. My father, at the age of twenty-nine, while working for Illinois Bell, lost his right arm in a freak accident. He was seated on a commuter car, with one elbow on the ledge of an open window, when a freight train came by, going the other way. Because of some carelessness, one door of a car was swinging free, and took off my father's arm with a swift, almost surgical slice. He got a small amount of insurance money, and, by implication, a lifetime job; but lost his chance to become an engineer, and thereafter did only clerical work with little advancement. Having to relearn writing with his left hand, he developed a strange signature, jagged, angular and backhand, which I found easy to forge on written excuses to our teachers when we were truants, which was often the case.

The climax came when we stayed home for almost two weeks, and, inevitably, a truant officer came to the door, suspicious of my notes. She was actually a pleasant young woman, but we were apprehensive. I even went so far, after being advised by phone that she was coming, as to apply talcum powder to our cheeks to make us look pale, wan and legitimately ill. It didn't work, and exposure to my father was certain and imminent.

Then came the scheme that should have brought the Fool-Killer down on me with lightning speed. It was nothing less than a fake suicide, with my unfortunate kid brother playing the risky lead role. It was inexcusable, and I still cringe thinking about it. It was, to begin with, uncalled for, since my father had not only never lifted a hand against us, but rarely even his voice. We were, it might be noted, not really bad, but rather passive on the whole, so there was no reason for any severe chastisements.

My imbecile notion was to make use of the gas stove, and go just far enough in a suicide attempt to divert my father's wrath from our misbehavior. In those days, gas was mainly carbon monoxide, which could bring unconsciousness quickly when inhaled.

My brother was doubtful and justifiably apprehensive, but I convinced him he'd be out only for a moment, after which I'd turn off the stove and open the kitchen windows.

All went smoothly enough. I'd stuffed paper under the closed door, and the gas built up rapidly. I watched through the glass panel, and when Walter slumped, I dashed in to revive him, which took only a few moments. Then I phoned my father, telling him that my brother, afraid of his anger, had tried to kill himself. The poor man, horrified, rushed home. The mean trick worked; he never did reproach us seriously for the truancy. And it wasn't until years later that I realized the risk I'd imposed on Walter. Carbon monoxide is dangerous and unpredictable. It's quite possible that he might not have regained consciousness, and that even if he did, brain damage could have resulted. I can only assume that the Fool-Killer must have been distracted by an even better and more deserving target, missing me by an eyelash.

Almost any new second lieutenant would be likely to attract the Fool-Killer, but I gave him an especially good opening for the third time, at least, when I made a speech to about 900 bored enlisted men.

I was suckered into that chore gradually. First, a senior officer asked me to write a marching song in honor of the division's new general, whose name, I believe, was Gerhardt. The tune they suggested was one I'd never heard, or even heard of, since anything not by Mozart or played by a swing band was beyond my ken. This was "The Red River Valley," which seemed to me on a par with the mournful and revolting "You Are My Sunshine," a great favorite of the more bucolic (and alcoholic) noncoms. My lyrics had such lines as, "Our General's as good as ten; he'll win this war *without* his men!" and each stanza ended with what was said to be the division's motto: "Powder River, let 'er buck!"

Then later, as requested, I wrote a few humorous skits for officers' dance parties. Being devoutly antisocial, even then, I didn't attend, so learned only by chance, from a friend, that the playlets were successful—and that the lieutenant in charge of entertainment had managed to imply, without saying so, but omitting any mention of my name, that he had created them. I took no action, because it would be too much trouble, make waves, and because I'd dashed the skits off and didn't think they were immortal literature.

As to the speech, having noted I was literate and rather glib, thanks to a few years of teaching, and probably had no fear of an audience, some top brass picked me to address the division, or much of it—I forget just how many were invited or would fit in the base theatre—about our relations with Russia, especially after the war. It was a time of some confusion. From being a sort of ally, the U.S.S.R. had suddenly made a non-aggression pact with Germany, only to find herself under attack by the duplicitous Hitler. After that, Stalin was our good friend again. No wonder the troops were baffled.

My job—"If you choose to accept it, Lieutenant"; much choice I had!—was to shoot down the constant rumors that days after Germany surrendered, we'd be at war with Russia.

Well, I wrote the speech, and aware that ninety-nine percent of the listeners were far more interested in weekend passes or whether they'd get K.P. duty soon than international relations, I added as much humor as I could, aping Mark Twain, or so I hoped.

I'd explain the battles going on in Russia, drawing on classified material, as if I knew something about it, which was not the case. I got my laughs, but the stretches in between were, I fear, rather deadly. But what set me up for the Fool-Killer was my closing peroration: "If anybody tells you that after the war we'll be fighting Russia—don't you believe it!"

Looking back on forty years of cold-to-warm war with the Soviets, I think I was a fool.

In 1965, after several decades of apartment living, much of it with my father and three brothers, I found myself in a rustic cottage on several acres of wooded grounds in the Garrapata area. There was electricity and a phone, but no gas, the only heat coming from a wood stove. I was completely ignorant of such rural living, but soon learned, with some dismay, that after every storm, even a small one, the power conked out, and, like as not, the phone. In addition, adding to my annoyance, the spring from which my water came would silt up, having to be cleared with a shovel. And it might be coffee-colored for days. If the storm was a fairly big one, the creek rose enormously, and I couldn't get the car over it to reach the highway.

All of that was frustrating, but didn't alert the Fool-Killer. He should have been drawn to my stove, which the agent who sold me the property must have assumed I understood. With no experience or instruction, I loaded it with far too much wood, much of it punky stuff I carried back from my long walks. Although there was a fire screen, it didn't stop all the sparks, and at times the vastly overloaded stove sent flames out through the chimney over the roof. I was too ignorant to notice that or draw any conclusions. I'd even go out for hours, with the huge blaze merrily augmenting. Why the house didn't burn down I'll never know, but the Fool-Killer missed his best chance of that decade, at least.

Surely much foolishness results from a combination of complacency and overconfidence. That was the case with me last summer. After decades of living in Chicago's hot, humid summers, I was a fanatical hater of such weather, preferring anything under sixty degrees. For years in Pacific Grove, when the nights got at all warm, or even when they didn't, but I wanted to cool off the house against a sticky day to come, I would leave both front and rear doors open, except for the flimsy screened ones, locked by the usual hook-and-eye only. I'd never heard of any forcible entries here, and only rarely in Monterey and Seaside, hence the complacency. Besides, as I'd done for years in Chicago and Los Angeles, I kept a handgun by my bed, an old, but serviceable Colt .38 Super Auto, well oiled, and loaded, but not cocked.

Well, on a muggy night, about one a.m., I became aware that a noisy party of some kind was in progress in a big house across the street, a building that seemed to have a flow of odd, strange looking, not to say *louche*, people. Although annoyed at the tumult and loud music, I managed to doze off again.

I was awakened more abruptly by a loud hammering at the front screen door, but assuming it was a drunk from the party, decided to just ignore the pest, figuring he'd get tired of it and leave.

The pounding continued, and suddenly, to my complete surprise and dismay, I realized the lock had been forced, and two intruders were in the house, and only a few yards from my bedroom. It was a man and a woman, and I heard her say in a low voice, "Maybe they're upstairs."

With a stentorian yell of "Who's there?" I grabbed my automatic, cocked it, and loped towards the front room where the two crazies were. Apparently as startled as I, they must have fled, because I got not even a glimpse of them, and found only the open doors. Whether they were drunk, deranged, or drugged, I'm not likely to know, it seems. And there was no point in calling the police, since I couldn't identify them, or even specify clothing, builds, or anything else of use to law officers.

The three of us, some might say, were lucky. Had they not fled, leaving an open, unlocked screen door, I could have been moved to shoot, since I knew nothing of their motives or intent. It's barely possible that if sufficiently incapacitated by drugs or booze, they somehow mistook my house for that of a friend, who would welcome, or excuse their brash entrance. And if I had shot, very likely one or both would be dead, for the Colt .38 Super Auto puts out a big, fast, deadly slug. After that, obviously, I might be in almost as much trouble—with the law, although I suspect any jury of reasonable people would not convict me in the circumstances. Caught in bed, I had no time to run or phone the police, so quickly were they closing in on me. Still, trials are dicey affairs, and who knows but that I'd have ended up in prison.

Since then, cured of that particular foolishness, I put better locks on my doors, and even secure both gates at sunset, although anybody taller than a dwarf could obviously step over the sagging, low fence. But another break-in would be much harder, and make a lot more noise, giving me time to decide whether to fight or flee. However, all has been quiet since, so I must conclude that the Fool-Killer missed another chance by being busy elsewhere—perhaps in Washington, where Congress and the White House surely qualify as nice game preserves for him.

Since few human interactions are ever really simple, it occasionally happens that some unlucky wight, who seems to be a prime target for the Fool-Killer, is actually a victim of fools. That was once the case with me. As an Officer Candidate, I was temporarily in charge of a field artillery battery—four 105mm howitzers. In the middle of my stint, the command came down: "Measure the adjusted compass."

I was delighted, since, thanks to my years at college, I was a trained student, and while diligently going through the field manual on the conduct of fire, had noted an interesting distinction. Here was a chance to show off, I thought, and set about the rather complicated procedure, which involved various settings of the sights, and readings of dials. As I busied myself with such tasks, I became aware of suppressed mirth—barely—among the spectators, a gaggle of captains, majors and light colonels.

Puzzled, I stared at them, and then the laughter became audible. A major set me straight. There was no need for all the measures and numbers; the command meant only that I read one simple setting. For a moment I was bewildered and chagrined, then enlightenment came. There were two commands, one to measure the adjusted compass, the other to report it. I had properly responded to the one given me, but these idiots, obviously unfamiliar with the subtle distinction, thought they had ordered the other. In vain I protested and argued; all assumed I'd blundered, complicating needlessly a simple command. Even the manual didn't convince them—it was obvious, they implied, that the more complicated order was almost never used, and I should have disregarded the command as given— incorrectly.

Well, it could be asserted that I was truly a fool, for who but a fool attempts to reason with bigger fools? Enough said!

There were many minor, trivial brushes with the Fool-Killer. As a boy of fifteen, vacationing in Wisconsin, I had access to a cheap, single-shot .22 rifle, and did a lot of plinking. Unfortunately, I knew absolutely nothing about firearms or the surprisingly potent little slugs, so neat, shiny and innocent looking. My worst sin was shooting at debris in the lake. The lead pellets would ricochet off the water, whining like banshees, and end up in the woods on the opposite bank. There were campers there, of course, but it never occurred to me that my bullets, distorted and tumbling, might well create havoc. Nothing like that happened, and the Fool-Killer spared me again.

And just out of high school, I got the zany idea that it would be fun to visit its library, restricted to students, and carefully monitored. The policy was to have all those working there to turn in a slip, which went to the "home room" teacher, who then certified that the user was indeed her charge. I blithely gave a fake name, overlooking the obvious consequences. Sure enough, a teacher came to the library, and relentlessly checked out all the names, one by one. I was soon matched up with the phony one, hustled off to the principal's office, and there brusquely interrogated. They did everything but take my fingerprints and a mug shot; my crime was officially recorded, and I was sternly warned never to try such a monkey trick again. It was a chastening experience, from which I should have learned—but fools are poor students.

Then there was the time when my kid brother and I, both under fifteen, were strolling on a mild summer evening in a business district of Chicago, and were approached by a man and woman, clean, but shabbily dressed. In a low, well modulated voice, seeming very downcast and ashamed, he told me that he and his wife had not eaten for thirty-six hours, and that while he hated to ask … no, not money; but could we buy them a little food at the market a few doors away? Overwhelmed and horrified by their plight, Walter and I pooled our few coins and bought them some staples: bread, milk, sausage and eggs. After they shambled out with the food, the merchant told us, rather condescendingly, that we'd been conned, that the couple made the rounds almost nightly, obtaining groceries and then apparently selling them at bargain prices to a regular clientele of willing purchasers. In short, a veritable network of people with at best dubious ethics. It didn't occur to the merchant that he was guilty himself; perhaps he'd have told us that if he didn't let them buy from him, there were other grocery stores on the street that would. Well, in this case, I can't help feeling, the Fool-Killer might have preferred us to the people who did the dirty work. It may be better to be a fool than a villain.

Incidentally, it should be noted that we fools have never been in short supply, or are likely to be in the future. In fact, the very fabric of our society, and most others, would unravel without us. We sustain the rogues, elect the weaseling, gutless legislators who frame our imbecile laws; and finance a host of layabouts. The sellers of trashy, short-lived goods; the publishers of garish magazines about ephemeral celebrities; the clothes designers—especially those for women, poor souls!—batten upon us with smug insolence. Astrologers, health-quacks, lottery promoters, and political-conspiracy fanatics need us desperately if they are to flourish and grow rich. Hate-mongers of all sorts, exploiting race, religion and class, sow discord among us for their own devious ends, and we cooperate, not just passively, but with febrile enthusiasm. Remember, too, that it takes at least twenty average fools to support one thoroughgoing scoundrel. And one nationwide chain-letter scam can use up—temporarily, since the mighty Fountain of Folly never slows—thousands of the best fools available. How many more are being sucked into the idiot-whirlpool of Ramtha and "channeling," who can say?

An interesting aspect of folly is that it frequently coexists quite happily with great intelligence and originality in a different field of knowledge. We all know people who are brilliant in some art or profession, but absolute nitwits on other subjects. The fault is not simple ignorance, which is common and reasonable—nobody, in this enormously complex world, can be an expert on everything—but the arrogance of pontificating, without adequate data, as if indeed thoroughly informed—positive about things, which as Ambrose Bierce defined it, means "wrong at the top of one's voice."

The best illustration of genius and folly in one body may be the remarkable case of Michel Chasles (1793-1880), a distinguished French geometer, who between 1861 and 1869 is thought to have paid about 150,000 francs for a number of forged letters. They were the work of one Denis Vrain-Lucas, a far-from-bright con man, who miraculously found an even bigger fool than himself. The holographic frauds were from such famous people as Shakespeare, Plato, Dante, Rabelais, Vergil, Sappho, Alexander the Great, Pompey and Cleopatra—a chatty note from her to Julius Caesar about their son, Caesarion. There was one from Lazarus to St. Peter, another by Mary Magdalene, and Vrain-Lucas actually hoped to sell his dupe the manuscript of the Sermon on the Mount, presumably in the hand of Jesus Christ. The geometer published in a scientific journal a letter supposedly by Pascal, in which he "proves" to have made most of the vital discoveries usually attributed to Newton. But the clincher is—can you believe this?—all the letters were in contemporary French! This silly fellow, a splendid research mathematician, refused for years to admit he'd been taken in.

And a student of folly might profit from a second, probing scrutiny of Mr. Ebenezer Scrooge. I like him no better after his hasty reformation than before it. In both states of being he was a fanatical sort of fool, an all-too-common variety. First, he's selfish, stingy, nasty, gloomy and unswervingly a free enterpriser, shouting the battle cry of Milton Friedman before that sage was born. Then, doing a lightning flip-flop, he's suddenly benevolent to the point of mawkishness, over-genial, and full of a moronic, undiscriminating love of children, old ladies, laughter, rich food, parties, and—Ah! Sweet Mystery of Life.

To me, this suggests those pitiable lost souls, with no rudders of their own, who leave an authoritative church, say, feeling somehow misplaced, only to join a series of even more repressive groups, right or left, and often end up as knee-jerk communists, happy to take direction and orders from the Big Marxist Daddies in Moscow. Had Dickens continued Scrooge's story honestly, I fear that the old man might have joined the Moonies or perished at Jonestown. For that sort of fool, it's just a matter of going from one rigid ideology to another, and never the balanced, sane, moderate approach to the vexations of life.

And finally, lest some of us get a little smug about our own wisdom, consider this trenchant observation by one Charles Caleb Colton (1777-1832), an eccentric English clergyman:

> The wise man has his follies no less than the fool; but it has been said that herein lies the difference—the follies of the fool are known to the world, but are hidden from himself; the follies of the wise are known to himself, but hidden from the world.

Surely this was a wise man, you are thinking—but not so fast! Faced with an operation, he killed himself; a minister committing suicide; is that wise or foolish? Well, remember this was just before the discovery by Morton and Long of anesthesia, when any serious surgery was an unspeakably dreadful ordeal. If you had to have, let's assume, your gall bladder removed, or a leg amputated while fully conscious, might not a quick, painless death seem preferable? Since I don't know what kind of operation was necessary, I have no opinion. In any case, even omitting Colton from our suspects, it's clear that the Fool-Killer has his work cut out for him, now and forever.

About the Author

Arthur Porges was born in Chicago, Illinois on August 20, 1915. One of four brothers, he was educated at Roosevelt High School and Senn High School before enrolling at The Lewis Institute where he achieved a Bachelor of Science Degree in Mathematics. After the successful completion of his postgraduate studies, through which he attained Masters Degrees in Mathematics and Engineering from the Illinois Institute of Technology, Porges enlisted in the U.S. Army in 1942. During the Second World War he served as an artillery instructor, teaching algebra and trigonometry to field personnel. He was stationed at various military installations including Camp White in Oregon, Fort Sill, Oklahoma, Camp Roberts, California and at Barnes Hospital in Vancouver, Washington. After the war Porges returned to Illinois and taught mathematics at the Western Military Academy, going on to serve as an assistant professor at De Paul University. Having taught at Occidental College in Los Angeles for a brief stint in the late forties, Porges made a permanent move to California in 1951 and spent several years as a mathematics teacher at Los Angeles City College. During this period he wrote and sold short stories as a sideline. In 1957, Porges retired from teaching to write full time. He went on to publish hundreds of short stories in numerous magazines and newspapers. Many of his stories appeared in *Alfred Hitchcock's Mystery Magazine*, *Ellery Queen's Mystery Magazine*, *Amazing Stories* and *The Magazine of Fantasy and Science Fiction*. His fiction spanned several genres, with tales ranging from science fiction and fantasy to horror, mysteries, and so on. At his most prolific his work was appearing in three or four periodicals in one month alone. Among his best-known stories are "The Ruum," "The Rats," "No Killer Has Wings," "The Mirror" and "The Rescuer." Fourteen book collections of his short stories have been published: *Three Porges Parodies and a Pastiche* (1988), *The Mirror and Other Strange Reflections* (2002), *Eight Problems in Space: The Ensign De Ruyter Stories* (2008), *The Adventures of Stately Homes and Sherman Horn* (2008), *The Calabash of Coral Island and Other Early Stories* (2008), *The Miracle of the Bread and Other Stories* (2008), *The Devil and Simon Flagg and Other Fantastic Tales* (2009), *The Curious Cases of Cyriack Skinner Grey* (2009), *The Ruum and Other Science Fiction Stories* (2010), *The Rescuer and Other Science Fiction* Stories (2014), *Unusual Plants of the Galaxy* (2014), *No Killer Has Wings: The Casebook of Dr. Joel Hoffman* (2017), *These Daisies Told: The Casebook of Professor Ulysses Price Middlebie* (2018) and *The Price of a Princess: Hardboiled Crime Fiction* (2020). A keen birdwatcher and an avid reader, in later years Porges wrote many articles, essays and poems, most of which were published in *The Monterey County Herald*. Several of his poems were collected in the book *Spring, 1836: Selected Poems* (2008). After spells in Laguna Beach and San Clemente, Porges moved north, eventually settling in Pacific Grove. He passed away, at the age of 90, in May 2006.

www.ingramcontent.com/pod-product-compliance
Lightning Source LLC
Chambersburg PA
CBHW050517260626
47157CB00004B/1361